Amy's TABLE

food for family & friends

Amy's TABLE

food for family & friends

BY AMY TOBIN

ORANGE FRAZER PRESS
Wilmington, Ohio

ISBN 978-1933197-39-5

Additional copies of *Amy's Table: Food for Family and Friends* may be ordered directly from:

Orange Frazer Press
P.O. Box 214
Wilmington, OH 45177

Telephone 1.800.852.9332 for price and shipping information.
Website: www.orangefrazer.com

Cover design: Jeff Fulwiler
Book design: Jeff Fulwiler and Chad DeBoard

Library of Congress Cataloging-in-Publication Data

Tobin, Amy, 1962-
 Amy's table : food for family and friends / by Amy Tobin.
    p. cm.
 ISBN 978-1-933197-39-5
 1. Cookery, American. I. Title.
 TX715.T6185 2007
 641.5973--dc22

                         2007023762

Printed in China

For my mother and father who nourished me with love, attention, thought—and food!

ackowledgements

Thanks to everyone who helped in the creation of this book. To Rob, Sean, and Katie—I love you. To my sisters and brothers Julie, Jenny, Carol, Johnny, and David and all the meals we shared at our family table. To Kate Gallion for her beautiful sense of style and Ryan Kurtz for his stunning photos—what a professional! To Ken Lewis for building the beautiful EQ. To Patti Marshall for encouraging and challenging me while being a great friend. To DC Stanfa for the divine meeting that led to this book. To Jon Stiles for being such a great supporter—and his marvelous wine pairings for the book. To Connie Volker for all the hard work, organization and detail handling required before we even got started. To Patrice Watson for her encouragement and shared love of big ideas. To Michelle Wylie for her incredible culinary skill, feedback, ideas, and hard work throughout the whole process. To the EQ staff, especially Grover Arnold, Jay "What's Shakin" Dickerson, Jacob Perry, and Jean Strasser for sticking with me for the long haul. To my "Boys" John Cobey and Dan Mawer for invaluable wisdom, guidance and advice. Cheers

introduction

Amy's Table: Food for Family and Friends is a reflection of my life at home, at the cooking school, and on radio and TV. It's a reflection of my wonderful family, best-ever staff and instructors and others who give me ideas and inspiration every single day. It's a reflection of the way I cook for my family and friends. And most of all, it's a reflection of love for my mother, who I lost to breast cancer, and for my sister, who survived. This book is for them and for all those whose lives have been touched by breast cancer. I'm honored to donate all proceeds from the sale of this book to the Susan G. Komen Foundation. To those of you who buy *Amy's Table* thanks, from the bottom of my heart, for your help in finding a cure.

SUSAN G.
komen
FOR THE **cure** GREATER CINCINNATI

For additional recipes, ideas and tips,
visit www.amystable.com

table of contents

Breakfast

LEMON BUTTERMILK WAFFLES with Blueberry Sauce — 2
BAKED CINNAMON APPLE PANCAKE — 4
FRUIT AND NUT GRANOLA — 6
SPICY BREAKFAST BURRITOS — 8
TEQUILA-SPIKED FRUIT SALAD with Lime — 10
CINNAMON SUGAR CHURROS — 12
CHERRY BUTTER — 14
FRUIT FLOWER KABOBS in Wheat Grass — 16

Hors d'Oeuvres

SEARED PEPPERED TUNA with Pickled Cucumber — 20
WINE GLAZED BRIE with Flower Petal Mosaic — 22
ASIAN CHICKEN SALAD on Endive Spears — 24
SMOKED SALMON PUFF PASTRY PIZZA with Capers and Dill — 26
ROSEMARY ROAST BEEF CROSTINI — 28
MINI RUEBENS in Rye Cups — 30
BOURSIN-FILLED PEPPADEWS — 32
GARDEN VEGETABLE BASKET — 34

Soups, Salads and Sides

TORTILLA SOUP with Creamy Cornbread and Honey Butter — 38
ITALIAN WEDDING SOUP with Great Garlic Bread — 40
BLACK BEAN with Bacon Soup — 42
SPINACH SALAD with Red Currant Dressing, Gorgonzola and Sweet and Spicy Nuts — 44
SOUTHERN SHRIMP SALAD — 46
CHOP-CHOP SALAD — 48
ROASTED RED SKIN AND GREEN BEAN SALAD — 50
ROUGH-CUT COLE SLAW with Blue Cheese — 52
MUSHROOM POTATOES — 54
GRILLED CORN with Roasted Garlic Butter — 56
CREAMED SPINACH — 58
SEASONED ONION STRAWS — 60

Entrées

OPEN FACED RATATOUILLE SANDWICHES with Gruyere   *64*
STUFFED ITALIAN SANDWICH   *66*
SALMON IN PHYLLO with Lemon and Herbs   *68*
SEAFOOD STEW   *70*
CREOLE PASTA   *72*
BAKED MACARONI AND CHEESE with Buttered Crumb Topping   *74*
CHICKEN AND BLACK BEAN ENCHILADAS
   with Rose's Green Salsa and Guacamole   *76*
ROSE'S GREEN SALSA AND GUACAMOLE   *78*
CHICKEN PICCATTA   *80*
MACADAMIA CHICKEN with Mango Butter Sauce   *82*
BBQ CHICKEN PIZZA   *84*
ASIAN BBQ RIBS   *86*
BEEF TENDERLOIN with Horseradish Sauce   *88*
BEEF TENDERLOIN STEW   *90*
BEEF FAJITAS with Peppers and Onions   *92*
CHILI with Sausage and Beef   *94*
MUSTARD PORK TENDERLOIN with Cherry Cabernet Sauce   *96*

Desserts

LEMON PANNA COTTA with Berry Sauce   *100*
PEACHES IN WINE   *102*
FRUIT TART with Gingersnap Cookie Crust   *104*
CHERRY ALMOND APRICOT TART   *106*
ALMOND SHORTCAKE with Double Cream and Triple Berries   *108*
SPICED PUMPKIN PIE with Bourbon Cream   *110*
CARAMEL CREPES with Brandied Caramel Sauce and Toasted Pecans   *112*
BUTTERMILK BANANA CAKE with Cream Cheese Cloud Frosting   *114*
CREAMY CHEESECAKE   *116*
DOUBLE CHOCOLATE MOUSSE TART with Chocolate Cookie Crust   *118*
CHOCOLATE BOWLS and Raspberry Sauce   *120*
ICE BOWLS with Sorbet   *122*
LIMONCELLO   *124*

Index

126

food for family & friends

breakfast

My morning routine is so important to me. My husband brings me coffee and the paper in bed and I spend nearly an hour reading, doing puzzles and sipping my beloved coffee before even stepping foot out of bed. It's indulgent—and a really great way to start the day. Every now and then I realize that if I had the same dedication to a morning work out I would be incredibly fit. Oh well. But I do make a point to eat a healthy breakfast. Most of the recipes in this chapter are better suited for a leisurely weekend breakfast, but I eat the Fruit and Nut Granola nearly every weekday morning. And the Breakfast Burritos are a school-day staple for my kids. Here's to the first great meal of the day!

LEMON BUTTERMILK WAFFLES with Blueberry Sauce — 2

BAKED CINNAMON APPLE PANCAKE — 4

FRUIT AND NUT GRANOLA — 6

SPICY BREAKFAST BURRITOS — 8

TEQUILA-SPIKED FRUIT SALAD with Lime — 10

CINNAMON SUGAR CHURROS — 12

CHERRY BUTTER — 14

FRUIT FLOWER KABOBS in Wheat Grass — 16

LEMON BUTTERMILK *Waffles* with Blueberry Sauce
[Makes 8 4-inch waffles]

prep time: 30 minutes   **cook time:** about 7 minutes

Make ahead: Both the Blueberry Sauce and the waffle batter can be made the night before; refrigerate until ready to use. Bake the waffles as directed and re-heat sauce over low heat.

Tip: For Gingerbread Waffles with Peach Sauce replace the poppy seeds and lemon peel in the waffle batter with 1 teaspoon each cinnamon and ground ginger and ¼ teaspoon ground cloves. For the sauce, replace the blueberries with drained canned peaches and the lemon juice with ½ teaspoon each cinnamon and ground ginger.

1 cup flour
¼ cup sugar
1 tablespoon poppy seeds
2 teaspoons baking powder
1 teaspoon baking soda
½ teaspoon salt
2 eggs, separated
1 cup buttermilk
2 teaspoons almond extract
¼ cup butter, melted
2 tablespoons lemon zest

Preheat waffle iron according to manufacturer's directions. In a large bowl whisk together the flour, sugar, poppy seeds, baking powder, baking soda and salt. In another bowl whisk together the egg yolks, buttermilk, almond extract, melted butter and lemon zest. In the bowl of an electric mixer beat the egg whites until stiff but not dry.

Add buttermilk mixture to flour mixture; whisk just until blended. Gently fold in egg whites; mix just until combined. Let batter rest 15 minutes before baking. Ladle batter into heated waffle iron. Cook until golden brown, about 7 minutes. Repeat with remaining batter.

BLUEBERRY SAUCE:

1 16-ounce package frozen blueberries, thawed, undrained
½ cup water
½ cup sugar
1 tablespoon cornstarch mixed with 2 tablespoons water
2 tablespoons lemon juice

In a medium saucepan combine the blueberries, water and sugar; bring to a boil. Simmer 15 minutes. In a small bowl combine cornstarch and water; stir into blueberry mixture. Add lemon juice. Bring to a boil; cook and stir 1 minute or until thickened. Cool slightly. Serve with waffles.

BAKED CINNAMON *Apple* PANCAKE

[Serves 4–6]

prep time: 20 minutes | **bake time:** 25 minutes

This wonderfully puffy pancake is something my sister Julia used to make for me. Try it for dessert with a scoop of vanilla or cinnamon ice cream.

Make ahead: No

Tip: You can add thinly sliced apple to the batter, too.

3 large eggs
¾ cup milk
¾ cup flour
½ teaspoon salt
¼ teaspoon cinnamon
1½ tablespoons butter

FILLING

¼ cup butter
5–6 baking apples, peeled, cored and sliced
¼ cup sugar
1½ teaspoons cinnamon
¼ teaspoon ground nutmeg
Pinch of salt

Garnish: Confectioners' sugar

Preheat oven to 450°F.

In a medium bowl beat the eggs, milk, flour, salt and cinnamon until smooth. In a heavy, ovenproof 12-inch skillet, melt the butter over medium high heat. When pan is hot, pour in the batter. Immediately place the skillet in the oven. Bake 15 minutes; reduce heat to 350°F and bake until the pancake is golden brown and puffy, about 10 minutes.

While the pancake is baking, melt butter in a sauté pan over medium heat. Add the apples, sugar, cinnamon, nutmeg and salt. Cook until just tender, about 8–10 minutes.

To serve: Slide the pancake onto a platter; top with the apple filling. Dust with confectioners' sugar. Slice into wedges and serve immediately.

FRUIT AND NUT *Granola*
[Makes 10 cups]

prep time: 15 minutes | *bake time:* 20 minutes

The recipe changes according to what I have in my cupboard and I constantly change up the nuts, fruits, and spices.

Make ahead: Keeps for a couple weeks in a large airtight canister.

Tip: I like to serve this with vanilla soymilk. Make a granola parfait by layering granola, yogurt and chopped fresh fruit in a parfait or wine glass.

6 cups old-fashioned oats (not instant)
1 cup shredded unsweetened coconut
2 cups nuts (sliced almonds, chopped walnuts or pecan pieces)
¼ cup flax seed or wheat germ
½ cup canola oil
½ cup honey
½ cup brown sugar
1 teaspoon almond extract
1 teaspoon vanilla extract
1 tablespoon pumpkin pie spice
1 teaspoon salt
2 cups dried fruit (chopped dates, raisins, golden raisins, cherries or cranberries)

Preheat oven to 325°F.

In a large bowl, mix the oats, shredded coconut, nuts and flax seed. In another bowl, whisk together the oil, honey, brown sugar, almond and vanilla extract, pumpkin pie spice and salt. Toss with the oat mixture; mix thoroughly. Divide mixture between 2 large rimmed baking sheets; spread in an even layer. Bake, stirring and tossing every 5 minutes, for 20 minutes or until golden brown. Cool completely. Transfer to a large mixing bowl; stir in the dried fruits. Store in an airtight container.

To serve: Serve with milk, soymilk or yogurt and a sprinkling of brown sugar if desired.

SPICY BREAKFAST *Burritos*

[Makes 6 large burritos]

prep time: 10 minutes | **bake time:** 10 minutes

Becky Long, The Kitchen Goddess, first introduced me to these Breakfast Burritos and the whole concept of freezing them. Breakfast hasn't been the same since! This is my spicier spin on Becky's recipe but I encourage you to play with it, too. You can replace the sausage with diced ham or crisply cooked bacon, or toss in some mushrooms—the variations are endless.

Make ahead: You can make these ahead in quantity and freeze them. Pull them from the freezer as needed for a quick and delicious breakfast.

Tip: Serve with Tequila Spiked Fruit Salad and Churros for a fun brunch.

6 eggs
½ pound chorizo (or bulk breakfast sausage) cooked and drained
¼ cup salsa
6 flour tortillas (try one of the flavored varieties)
1 cup shredded Pepper Jack cheese

Garnish: Additional salsa, sour cream, chopped cilantro

Heat a large non-stick skillet over medium low heat. Beat eggs; add to skillet. Cook, stirring frequently, until set. Add cooked sausage and salsa to egg mixture; mix gently.

Warm tortillas as directed on package. Divide egg and sausage mixture between tortillas; sprinkle with cheese. Roll up each tortilla to make burritos. Serve immediately with salsa, sour cream and cilantro or freeze as directed below.

To Freeze: Place prepared burritos on cookie sheets; freeze until solid. Wrap individually; package in zip-lock freezer bags.

To thaw/serve: When you're ready to eat them, unwrap the burritos, wrap loosely in microwave safe paper towel and heat in the microwave on high power for 1–3 minutes until hot and cheese is melted.

seize

the

day

TEQUILA-SPIKED *Fruit* SALAD with Lime

[Serves 6]

prep time: 20 minutes

This fruit salad makes a great brunch dish and is wonderful with grilled fish or chicken. You can always leave out the tequila or replace it with 1 teaspoon vanilla extract.

Make ahead: The dressing can be made a day ahead. The fruit can be dressed and chilled for up to several hours. Add the banana just before serving.

4 tablespoons honey
3 tablespoons frozen limeade concentrate, thawed
2 tablespoons tequila
2 cups cantaloupe, peeled and cut into chunks
2 cups honeydew melon, peeled and cut into chunks
2 cups seedless red or green grapes, cut in half
2 cups pineapple, peeled and cut into chunks
2 firm bananas, peeled and sliced
1 cup strawberries, hulled and halved

Garnish: Lime zest

In a large bowl whisk together the honey, limeade and tequila. Mix in fruit.

To serve: Garnish with lime zest.

CINNAMON SUGAR *Churros*

[Serves 6]

prep time: 20 minutes | **bake time:** 3–4 minutes

I first had these little Mexican doughnuts in Texas. It was love at first bite. The salt in the cinnamon sugar is what makes them addicting.

Make ahead: Dough can be made 2–3 hours ahead. Cover; store at room temperature until ready to cook.

Tip: Nutmeg loses its intensity faster than most spices. For best flavor, buy whole nutmeg and grate it as needed using a microplane grater.

CINNAMON SUGAR

1 cup sugar mixed with 2 teaspoons cinnamon and ½ teaspoon salt

BATTER

1 cup whole milk
¼ cup (½ stick) unsalted butter
2 teaspoons sugar
½ teaspoon cinnamon
¼ teaspoon nutmeg
½ teaspoon sea salt
1 cup flour
4 large eggs
Oil as needed for frying

In a heavy saucepan combine milk, butter, sugar, cinnamon, nutmeg and salt; bring to a boil, stirring until sugar dissolves and butter melts. Reduce heat to medium-low. Add flour; stir with a wooden spoon until a shiny dough forms, about 1 minute. Transfer to the bowl of an electric mixer; cool 5 minutes.

Beat in eggs, one at a time. Continue beating until a smooth, shiny, sticky paste forms. Spoon batter into a pastry bag fitted with a large star tip.

Pour oil to the depth of 2–3 inches in a large heavy skillet over medium-high heat; heat to 350°F. Working in batches, pipe batter into 4-inch-long ribbons. Cut the lengths using scissors, carefully letting them slide into the hot oil. Fry until brown, about 2 minutes per side. Transfer to paper towels. Cool 5 minutes.

To serve: Toss in cinnamon sugar to coat. Serve warm.

CHERRY *Butter*

For a really nice addition to almost any breakfast bread, try serving this sweet-tart cherry butter. Wonderful on toast, English muffins, pancakes or popovers, you can easily change up the flavor by choosing a different flavor preserve.

Make ahead: The butter needs to chill for several hours to firm back up. Can be made ahead; keep covered and refrigerated, for several days.

Tip: For good texture, make sure to have the butter and cream cheese at room temperature.

4 tablespoons unsalted butter, at room temperature
4 ounce cream cheese, at room temperature
¼ cup confectioners' sugar
½ teaspoon almond extract
¼ cup cherry preserves (or your favorite flavor)

In a food processor or electric mixer combine the butter, cream cheese, confectioners' sugar and almond extract; blend well. Pulse in the cherry preserves just until combined. Transfer to a serving bowl or crock; chill, covered, until ready to serve.

change

is

good

FRUIT FLOWER *Kabobs* in Wheat Grass

Food that has a sense of humor is just more fun to eat. These little flowers make an adorable centerpiece or use them as tiny "flower gardens" at each guest's place. Kids love them.

Make ahead: The fruit can be sliced up to one day ahead. Cover and refrigerate until ready to cut into shapes. The flower shapes can be cut several hours in advance; refrigerate until ready to assemble. The flowers should be assembled no more than 30 minutes ahead. Refrigerate the entire bouquet until ready to serve. Keep additional skewers, inserted upright into floral foam, in the refrigerator and replenish as needed.

Tip: The flowers generate a lot of scraps; use them to make Tequila-spiked Fruit Salad with Lime

Cantaloupe, peeled and sliced into ⅓-inch thick slices
Honeydew, peeled and sliced into ⅓-inch thick slices
Star fruit, cut into ⅓-inch thick slices
Raspberries, blueberries, red and green grapes or melon balls
Flower-shaped canapé cutters or small cookie cutters
Wooden skewers
Wheat grass

After peeling the melons, cut ⅓-inch thick slices from each long side. Once you've reached the seed-filled center, start slicing off each short end. Continue slicing until you've reached the center. Discard the centers and seeds. Using assorted sizes of flower shaped canapé or cookie cutters, cut flower shapes from the melon slices. Reserve any scraps for another use.

To assemble: Slide a blueberry onto a wooden skewer (this will stop the fruit flowers from sliding down the skewer). Slide a large flower shape or slice of star fruit on the skewer. Slide a smaller flower shape on the skewer. Cover the tip of the skewer with a raspberry, blueberry, grape half or melon ball. Insert the completed flower into a small flat of wheat grass. Repeat with remaining melon and fruit. Refrigerate until ready to serve.

To be "party-ready" keep your cupboard stocked using this very basic list. Each time you're ready to shop, take a quick peek to see what needs replenishing.

- Mixed nuts
- An assortment of gourmet crackers, flatbreads, bread sticks and tortilla chips
- A few great cheeses
- Salsa, tapenades, spreads and chutneys
- Jars of olives, roasted red peppers, and marinated artichoke hearts

hors d'oeuvres

When I think of the fussy hors d'oeuvres I used to make I literally cringe. As a busy working mom, complicated entertaining just doesn't fit into my life. My new philosophy on hors d'oeuvres is that they should be simple, tasty and work equally well in both formal and casual settings.

Some of the most memorable moments in our lives are the simple, spontaneous ones—like friends dropping by unannounced. Consider being prepared for spontaneity—and planning ahead for the unexpected. With just a little planning you can pull off any gathering with style. It starts by making sure your guests feel welcome, comfortable, and absolutely central to the good time, and staying focused on the notion that the very best parties all share the same simple ingredients—good food and a good mood.

Impromptu entertaining is easy if you keep a few key items on hand. Good food that you can put together easily. Food that will impress and satisfy your guests infinitely more than watching you work yourself senseless over something complicated and fussy. I kid you not—I recently served waffle-cut potato chips with dip piped on them. Everyone loved them. I rest my case.

Remember that presentation does so much for food, not to mention the overall feeling of a gathering. Keep it simple and try to enhance the characteristics of the food. Cheese is a natural food—play that up by using a natural looking serving piece. A slate tile, a wooden board or a rustic basket works great. Serve sushi or shrimp on glass trays or blocks, which mimic the feeling of the sea. Cake stands elevate and add immediate interest for even the most basic hors d'oeuvres. And use interesting bowls for nuts, olives, spreads and dips. Voila! Whether planned or impromptu, you'll be looking good—and your guests will be happy.

SEARED PEPPERED TUNA with Pickled Cucumber — 20

WINE GLAZED BRIE with Flower Petal Mosaic — 22

ASIAN CHICKEN SALAD on Endive Spears — 24

SMOKED SALMON PUFF PASTRY PIZZA with Capers and Dill — 26

ROSEMARY ROAST BEEF CROSTINI — 28

MINI RUEBENS in Rye Cups — 30

BOURSIN-FILLED PEPPADEWS — 32

GARDEN VEGETABLE BASKET — 34

SEARED PEPPERED *Tuna* with Pickled Cucumber

[Serves 8]

prep time: 30 minutes

Chef Paul Teal, a British chef, taught me this recipe. I love that it's equal parts elegance and simplicity—the best formula for any hors d'oeuvres. Speaking of simplicity—he also taught me the importance of understated presentation. When we were catering partners, I proudly showed him a parsley-laden hors d 'oeuvres tray that I had assembled. His response was, "It looks like bloody Central Park." He was right. Use lots of restraint when garnishing.

Make ahead: The tuna can be seared several hours in advance; refrigerate until ready to slice and serve. The cucumber can be pickled several hours in advance; refrigerate until ready to serve.

Tip: For a different look, dice the seared tuna and serve it in cucumber cups.

1 pound tuna, without skin, cut 1-inch thick
Coarsely ground black pepper, as needed to coat

PICKLED CUCUMBER

¼ cup sugar
¼ cup salt
½ cup white vinegar
2 cucumbers, peeled and very thinly sliced

Tuna: Cut the tuna into equal sized "logs". Roll and press each log in black pepper. Sear on all sides in a very hot pan; immediately refrigerate to cool. The inside should still be very rare.

Pickled cucumber: In a medium bowl whisk together the sugar and salt; stir in the cucumber slices. Let stand for 20 minutes. Drain; add the vinegar. When ready to serve remove cucumber slices with a slotted spoon.

To serve: Slice the tuna in ½-inch thick slices; top each with a piece of pickled cucumber. Serve immediately.

WINE GLAZED *Brie* with Flower Petal Mosaic
[Makes 2 8-inch wheels]

prep time: 30 minutes

I love pretty party food—and whimsical presentation.
The shimmery wine glaze over the delicate herbs and flower
petals makes simple wheels of Brie really special.

Make ahead: Brie can be assembled several hours in advance.

Tip: Prepare two small wheels of Brie instead of one large—that way you can whisk
away the nearly finished (and no longer as lovely) wheel and bring out another fresh
one. That's a good approach for all hors d'oeuvres.

2 8-ounce wheels of Brie
1 envelope unflavored gelatin
¼ cup cold water
2 cups dry white wine
Edible flower petals
Assorted herbs

In a small bowl stir the gelatin into the cold water; let stand 5 minutes.

In a saucepan over medium heat combine the white wine with the softened gelatin.
Heat and stir until the gelatin is dissolved. Remove from heat and cool, stirring.

Brush Brie with gelatin mixture. Arrange flower petals and herbs on top of the Brie in a
decorative (or completely free-form) pattern. Gently brush with the remaining gelatin
mixture; chill until set. Continue to brush with wine glaze and chill until the herbs and
flowers are completely encased in the wine glaze.

To serve: Serve with baguette slices, crackers and apple slices if desired.

ASIAN *Chicken* SALAD on Endive
Spears [Serves 4–6]

prep time: 20 minutes

Endive spears are a great vehicle for getting any number of tasty things into your mouth. Try the Southern Shrimp Salad served this way, too.

Make ahead: Asian Chicken Salad can be made several hours ahead. Assemble just before serving.

Tip: Buy the Belgian Endive no more than a day before you'll use them. Choose heads that are firm and compact with yellowish tips. Separate the leaves before gently washing them in cool water. Store them in the fridge, wrapped in paper towels then tucked in a Ziploc bag.

3 heads Belgian endive
1½ cups cooked chicken, finely diced or finely shredded
1 8-ounce can sliced water chestnuts, drained, finely chopped
¼ cup finely chopped celery
½ cup fresh cilantro, chopped
½ cup chopped peanuts

DRESSING

2 tablespoons soy sauce
2 tablespoons rice wine vinegar
1 tablespoon fresh ginger, peeled and minced
1 tablespoon sugar
1 tablespoon lime juice, or to taste
2 tablespoons sesame oil

Garnish: Finely sliced green onions, chopped peanuts and cilantro

Wash endive; separate spears. Chill until ready to assemble.

In a medium mixing bowl combine chicken, water chestnuts, celery, cilantro and peanuts. Set aside.

In a food processor or blender combine all dressing ingredients; toss with chicken mixture.

To serve: Spoon chicken mixture onto endive spears; garnish with cilantro, peanuts and green onions.

SMOKED *Salmon* PUFF PASTRY PIZZA with Capers and Dill Spears

[Makes 2 pizzas, serves 16]

prep time: 25 minutes | *bake time:* 15 minutes

Puff pastry is God's gift to people who like to entertain. Just about anything served on (or in) puff pastry tastes delicious.

Make ahead: The puff pastry can be topped with the cheese mixture several hours in advance. Refrigerate until ready to bake. Prep all the topping ingredients several hours in advance, too. Bake and assemble just before serving.

Tip: Make sure to let the goat cheese and cream cheese come to room temperature before mixing and spreading on the pastry.

1 sheet frozen puff pastry; thawed according to package instructions
4 ounces cream cheese, at room temperature
4 ounces goat cheese, at room temperature
1 tablespoon mayonnaise
4–6 ounces thinly sliced smoked salmon
¼ cup chopped red onion
2 tablespoons chopped fresh dill
1 tablespoon capers, drained
3 teaspoons lemon zest

Let puff pastry stand at room temperature for 30 minutes. Preheat oven to 400°F.
On a lightly floured surface, gently unfold pastry sheet. Roll into a 15x10-inch rectangle.
Cut in half lengthwise; prick each half all over and thoroughly with a fork. Transfer to a baking sheet.

In a medium bowl combine cream cheese, goat cheese and mayonnaise.
Spread ½ of cheese mixture onto each piece of pastry to within ½-inch of the edge.
Bake 15 minutes.

Remove from oven, top with salmon, red onion, dill, capers and lemon zest.

To serve: Cut each half into 8 pieces; transfer to a platter; serve.

ROSEMARY ROAST BEEF *Crostini*

[Makes about 20 pieces]

prep time: 30 minutes

Make ahead: The crostini can be made a day ahead; store in an airtight container. The beef can be mixed several hours in advance; refrigerate until ready to assemble. The topping can be made several days ahead; refrigerate until ready to serve.

Tip: Get a great quality rare roast beef thinly sliced at the deli. Cut the baguette on an angle for a larger, prettier crostini. When serving a cheese tray or dips, serve crostini in addition to crackers for a great looking display.

¼ cup olive oil
1 teaspoon garlic powder
½ teaspoon salt
½ teaspoon red pepper flakes
½ teaspoon freshly ground black pepper
2 teaspoons minced fresh rosemary leaves
1 pound thinly sliced rare roast beef, sliced into ⅓-inch wide strips

In a shallow dish combine the olive oil and seasonings. Add roast beef; toss to coat. Set aside while making crostini.

CROSTINI

½ cup olive oil or olive oil spray
Salt and pepper to taste
1 baguette sliced into ⅓-inch slices

Preheat oven to 350°F. Brush or spray both sides of bread slices with olive oil. Season with salt and pepper. Bake 10–12 minutes, or until golden brown and crisp.

TOPPING AND GARNISH

4-ounces cream cheese, softened
½ cup blue cheese dressing
¼ cup crumbled blue cheese plus more for garnish
Salt and pepper to taste
Chopped fresh Italian parsley

In the bowl of an electric mixer beat the cream cheese until smooth. Add dressing; beat until well blended. Stir in crumbled blue cheese by hand. Season with salt and pepper.

To serve: Top each crostini with some of the meat. Top with a dollop of blue cheese mixture. Sprinkle with additional crumbled blue cheese and chopped Italian parsley; serve.

This is a favorite of our cooking school students of EQ at The Party Source. If you're looking for an alternative to blue cheese, try a horseradish sauce.

MINI *Ruebens* in Rye Cups
[Makes 12]

prep time: 30 minutes

The Rye Cups are so simple—they're really just a variation on crostini—but they look like they took real effort. You can use a round cutter or cut the bread into squares before pressing it into the muffin cups.

Make ahead: Rye Cups can be baked a day ahead; store in an airtight container until ready to assemble. Filling can be made one day ahead; refrigerate until ready to assemble.

Tip: For a variation, use soft Italian bread. Spray with olive oil and sprinkle with parsley, salt and pepper. Use a rolling pin to embed the seasonings then bake as directed for the Rye Cups. Fill with finely shredded Romaine lettuce dressed with Caesar salad dressing. Garnish with Parmesan cheese.

12 slices soft rye bread, crusts removed
Olive oil spray
1 cup sauerkraut, well-drained
4 ounces cream cheese, cubed, at room temperature
½ cup Thousand Island Dressing, divided
½ pound thinly sliced deli corned beef, chopped
Shredded Swiss cheese
Finely diced dill pickle

Preheat oven to 350°F. Spray a 12 opening muffin tin with cooking spray. Spray both sides of slices of rye bread with olive oil spray; roll and press with a rolling pin to flatten slightly. Fit each bread slice into a muffin tin opening, forming a cup. Bake just until lightly browned and crisp, about 10 minutes. Cool.

In a medium bowl, whisk together the softened cream cheese and ¼ cup Thousand Island dressing.

To assemble: Place a spoonful of the cream cheese mixture in each rye cup. Top with a spoonful of sauerkraut, then corned beef. Drizzle the remaining dressing over the beef; garnish with shredded Swiss Cheese and finely diced dill pickle.

BOURSIN-FILLED *Peppadews*
[Serves 6]

prep time: **15 minutes**

Make ahead: Peppadews can be filled several hours ahead; refrigerate until ready to serve. Garnish just before serving.

1 14-ounce jar Peppadews (whole sweet piquant peppers, use mild or hot)
1 5.2-ounce box Boursin garlic and herb cheese, at room temperature

Garnish: finely chopped parsley

Drain the peppadews completely. Cut a small slice off the bottom of each to help it stand upright.

Place the room temperature Boursin in a small bowl; whisk until smooth. Transfer to a piping bag fitted with a star tip. Pipe (or spoon) some cheese into each peppadew. Refrigerate until ready to serve.

To serve: Garnish with finely chopped parsley.

GARDEN *Vegetable* BASKET

prep time: 15 minutes

Make ahead: The basket can be assembled several hours ahead. Wrap with plastic wrap and refrigerate until ready to serve.

Tip: The basket will be a bit precarious—don't try to run around town with it. Reserve some vegetables to mound on once you've placed it where you'll be serving it.

Like the Fruit Kebobs in Wheat Grass, this is simply an idea to make something very ordinary, like a veggie tray, extraordinary. There's no recipe here, just some inspiration. Use a beautiful basket and fill it with crumbled newspaper. This step elevates the vegetables and adds some drama. Line the entire basket with cabbage or kale leaves. (I usually wander through the produce section and pull off the outer leaves of cabbage that everyone throws away anyway. Yes, people think I'm weird.) Let some of the leaves hang over the edge of the basket. Then start mounding in your favorite vegetables. Bountiful is better—really pile them on. Take care to spread color and height evenly throughout the basket.

To serve: Serve with a selection of your favorite dips.

bountiful

is

better

soups, salads & sides

Soups

TORTILLA SOUP with Creamy Cornbread and Honey Butter   38

ITALIAN WEDDING SOUP with Great Garlic Bread   40

BLACK BEAN WITH BACON SOUP   42

Salads

SPINACH SALAD with Red Currant Dressing, Gorgonzola and Sweet and Spicy Nuts   44

SOUTHERN SHRIMP SALAD   46

CHOP-CHOP SALAD   48

ROASTED RED SKIN AND GREEN BEAN SALAD   50

ROUGH-CUT COLE SLAW with Blue Cheese   52

Sides

MUSHROOM POTATOES   54

GRILLED CORN with Roasted Garlic Butter   56

CREAMED SPINACH   58

SEASONED ONION STRAWS   60

TORTILLA *Soup*
[Serves 6–8]

This is one of those go-to soups my whole family loves. Serve it with Creamy Corn Bread and Honey Butter and Caramel Crepes with Toasted Pecans for dessert.

Make ahead: Soup can be made a day ahead; refrigerate until ready to serve. Tortilla strips are best made just before serving.

Tip: I like to bake my own tortilla chips. They taste terrific and I tend to eat fewer than when I open a big bag. Always use corn tortillas for homemade chips.

Cooking spray
8 6-inch corn tortillas
Salt
2 tablespoons olive oil
1 medium onion, chopped
2 cloves garlic, minced
2 cups cooked chicken, diced
1 can (15¼ ounces) whole kernel corn, drained
1 can (15 ounces) black beans, rinsed and drained
2 cups salsa
1 can (4 ounces) chopped green chilies
1 package (1¼ ounces) taco seasoning mix
1 32-ounce box chicken broth (4 cups)
Juice of ½ a lime
Salt and pepper to taste

Garnish: Sour cream, shredded Monterey Jack, finely chopped cilantro, tortilla strips, and lime slices

Preheat oven to 350°F. Spray a baking sheet and both sides of the corn tortillas with cooking spray. Using scissors or a pizza cutter, slice the tortillas into strips; sprinkle lightly with salt. Place on the prepared baking sheet; bake 12–15 minutes or until crisp and lightly browned. Set aside.

While the chips are baking, heat the olive oil in a heavy pot over medium high heat. Add the onions and garlic; sauté until the onions are soft. Add the chicken, corn, beans, salsa, chilis and taco seasoning; stir to combine. Add chicken broth; stir. Bring to a boil; reduce heat and simmer, 10–15 minutes. Stir in lime juice. Season with salt and pepper.

To serve: place a few tortilla strips into soup bowls; ladle soup over. Garnish with sour cream, shredded cheese, cilantro, remaining tortilla strips and a lime slice.

CREAMY CORN BREAD and Honey Butter
[Makes an 8x8-inch pan]

prep time: 10 minutes | **cook time:** 25–30 minutes

Make ahead: Corn bread tastes best straight from the oven.

1½ cups self-rising corn meal
2 tablespoons sugar
3 eggs
¾ cup canola oil
1 cup sour cream or plain low fat (not fat free) yogurt
1 cup buttermilk

Preheat oven to 350°F. Spray an 8x8-inch baking pan with cooking spray. In a large bowl combine the corn meal and sugar. In another bowl combine the eggs, oil, sour cream and buttermilk; whisk until well blended. Add the egg mixture to the dry ingredients; mix until combined. Pour into prepared pan. Bake 25–30 minutes or until lightly golden brown. Cool slightly.

HONEY BUTTER

There's nothing better than honey butter melting into warm corn bread, except maybe honey butter melting into a toasted English muffin!

1¼ cup butter, softened
½ cup honey

ITALIAN *Wedding* SOUP

[Serves 6]

prep time: 30 minutes | **cook time: 55 minutes**

I made this soup on the first episode of Amy's Table on CET. The crew loved it as much as my family does.

Make ahead: Soup can be made a day ahead; refrigerate until ready to reheat.
Tip: Make the tiny meatballs uniform in size so that they cook evenly. Use a tiny cookie scoop—or enlist a kid to help!

½ head escarole (about ½ pound or 4 cups chopped)
1 large carrot, chopped
12 cups chicken broth
4 ounces ditalini or tubetti, or other small pasta

Separate the escarole leaves and wash thoroughly to remove all grit. Stack the leaves; cut them crosswise into 1-inch strips. Combine the escarole, carrot and broth in a large pot. Bring to a simmer and cook until the escarole is almost tender, about 30 minutes.

MEATBALLS

½ pound of a combination of ground veal, pork and beef
½ cup plain dry bread crumbs
½ cup finely grated Parmesan cheese
½ cup grated onion
1 large egg
½ teaspoon salt
Freshly ground pepper, to taste

While the soup is simmering, combine the ground meat, bread crumbs, cheese, grated onion, egg, salt, and pepper in a medium bowl. Shape the mixture into tiny balls, less than 1 inch in diameter.

When the escarole is almost tender, stir in the pasta and return the soup to a simmer. Drop the meatballs into the soup. Cook over low heat, stirring gently, until the meatballs and pasta are cooked, about 20 minutes. Season with salt and pepper.

To serve: Garnish with freshly grated Parmesan cheese.

GREAT GARLIC BREAD
[Serves 4]

prep time: 15 minutes   *cook time:* 30 minutes

Make ahead:

Tip.

1 loaf Italian bread, cut in half lengthwise
4 cloves garlic
½ teaspoon salt
4 tablespoons unsalted butter, softened

To serve:

BLACK BEAN WITH *Bacon* SOUP
[Serves 4]

prep time: 15 minutes | **cook time:** 30 minutes

Make ahead: Can be made several days ahead and re-heated. Stir in the lime juice just before serving.

Tip: For chunky soup, add the second can of beans after the soup has been pureed. If you prefer a smoother soup, add all the beans at once and puree until smooth.

2 tablespoons olive oil
1 onion, chopped
3 slices bacon, diced
4 garlic cloves, minced
1 tablespoon ground cumin
1 jalapeño, seeded and chopped
2 15-ounce cans black beans, drained and rinsed, divided
1 15-ounce can diced tomatoes, with juice
1½ cups chicken broth
Juice of ½ a lime
Salt and pepper to taste

Garnish:
Sour cream
2 strips crisply cooked bacon, crumbled
Chopped fresh cilantro
Sliced green onions

Heat oil in heavy large pot over medium-high heat. Add onion, bacon and garlic; sauté until onions are soft. Stir in cumin and jalapeño. Add one can of beans, tomatoes with juice, and broth; bring to a boil. Reduce heat to medium, cover and cook 15 minutes. Using a stick blender puree' the soup (or transfer the soup to blender and puree until smooth. Return puree to pot). Stir in remaining can of beans. Simmer about 15 minutes. Stir in lime juice; season to taste with salt and pepper.

To serve: Ladle soup into bowls. Garnish with sour cream, crumbled bacon, cilantro and green onions.

SPINACH *Salad* with Red Currant Dressing, Gorgonzola and Sweet and Spicy Nuts

[Serves 4]

prep time: 25 minutes

Make ahead: The Red Currant Dressing and the Sweet and Spicy Nuts can be made one day ahead. Assemble the salad just before serving.

Tip: Turn this salad into an entrée by topping it with sliced grilled chicken or pork tenderloin. And the nuts are great on their own as a snack, too.

¼ cup red currant jelly
¼ cup cider vinegar
½ cup canola oil
8 cups baby spinach
½ sweet or red onion, peeled, cut in half and thinly sliced
½ cup Gorgonzola cheese, crumbled
Salt and pepper, to taste
Garnish: Sweet and Spicy Pecans

Place jelly and vinegar in a blender or food processor; add the oil in a steady stream. Process until well blended. Combine spinach, sliced onion and Gorgonzola in a large bowl; toss with dressing and season with salt and pepper. Garnish with Sweet and Spicy Nuts.

SWEET AND SPICY NUTS

[Makes 2 cups]

Spice mix:
1½ teaspoons salt
1½ teaspoons cumin
1 teaspoon hot pepper flakes
1 tablespoon sugar

3 tablespoons peanut oil
½ cup granulated sugar
2 cups nuts (use whole blanched almonds, cashews, walnuts, pecans, hazelnuts or macadamias)

In a shallow dish combine the spice mix ingredients; set aside.

Heat oil in a sauté pan over medium-high heat. Add nuts; sprinkle with sugar. Sauté until golden and caramelized, stirring frequently. Remove nuts with slotted spoon; toss with spice mix. Spoon onto a baking sheet; cool. Break apart to separate if needed.

SOUTHERN *Shrimp* SALAD

[Serves 6]

prep time: 20 minutes | **cook time:** 10 minutes

Make ahead: Best made several hours in advance. Can be made one day ahead; refrigerate until ready to serve.

Tip: Heating the mixture in the cooking water for 5 minutes or more makes the shrimp really flavorful. Use the same technique for shrimp cocktail. To get shrimp cocktail well-chilled for serving, place a Ziploc bag of ice in a shallow dish. Lay the shrimp on top of the ice-filled bag; cover and chill until ready to serve.

1 (3-ounce) bag Shrimp and Crab Boil
1 lemon cut in half
Salt
1½ pounds medium shrimp, shells on

DRESSING

½ cup mayonnaise
2 tablespoons fresh lemon juice plus more to taste
2 teaspoons Dijon mustard
¼ cup finely chopped sweet onion
1 tablespoon minced fresh parsley leaves
½ teaspoon garlic powder
A generous pinch cayenne pepper

1 cup finely chopped celery
2 tablespoons finely chopped chives
Salt and pepper to taste

Garnish: Chopped chives, lemon slices

Bring a medium pot of water to a boil with the crab boil bag, lemon halves, and a generous amount of salt. Boil 5 minutes. Add the shrimp; cook at a low boil for 2 minutes. Remove from heat; let stand 3 minutes. Drain. When the shrimp are cool enough to handle, peel and de-vein. Roughly chop the shrimp.

In a medium bowl, mix together dressing ingredients. Stir in the chopped shrimp, celery and chives. Season to taste with salt, pepper and additional lemon juice. Refrigerate until well chilled, about 2 hours.

To serve: Garnish with chopped chives and lemon slices.

Every time my family and I are in Florida we eat ourselves senseless on seafood salad. I love it on a slightly salty cracker—or right out of the fridge when no one's looking. The difference between this salad and the Florida stuff is that I don't add imitation crab. Add it if you'd like—I'm the first to admit it tastes good. A scoop of Southern Shrimp Salad on greens makes a nice lunch, or serve it on endive spears for a light hors d' oeuvre.

CHOP-CHOP *Salad*

[Serves 4]

prep time: 20 minutes

Make ahead: Dressing can be made several days in advance; refrigerate until ready to use.

Tip: The dressing for this salad is a great all-purpose vinaigrette. Double the recipe and keep it in the refrigerator to use as both a salad dressing and a marinade for meats.

DRESSING

½ cup balsamic vinegar
1 tablespoon Dijon mustard
2 tablespoons chopped fresh herbs or 1 tablespoon dried (use a mixture of basil, oregano and thyme)
½ cup olive oil
Salt and pepper to taste

1 head romaine lettuce, chopped
1 English cucumber; peeled and diced
¼ pound sliced salami, chopped
⅓ cup roasted red peppers (one 4 ounce jar), drained and chopped
⅓ cup red onion, chopped
½ cup ripe black olives, pitted and chopped
½ cup provolone cheese, diced

In the bowl of a blender or food processor, combine the vinegar, mustard and herbs. Process until well combined. With the motor running, add the oil in a steady stream. Season to taste with salt and pepper.

In a large bowl combine the chopped salad ingredients. Toss with dressing; serve.

ROASTED RED SKIN AND *Green Bean* SALAD

[Serves 4–6]

prep time: 25 minutes | **cook time:** 45 minutes | **chill time:** several hours/overnight

Make ahead: Tastes best made a day ahead.

Tip: Make this salad easily with a little advance prep. When roasting potatoes for another meal, roast extra. Blanch extra green beans when making another meal, too, and refrigerate until ready to assemble the salad.

2 pounds small red new potatoes, scrubbed and cut into quarters
Olive oil as needed
1 pound fresh green beans

DRESSING

¼ cup olive oil
¼ cup white wine vinegar
1 teaspoon sugar
1 clove garlic, minced
1 teaspoon salt
¾ cup mayonnaise
1 tablespoon fresh dill, chopped, plus more for garnish

⅓ cup chopped sweet onion
2 ribs celery, chopped
2 hard-boiled eggs, peeled and chopped
Salt and pepper

Preheat oven to 400°F.

In a rimmed baking sheet, toss potatoes with enough olive oil to lightly coat. Season generously with salt and pepper. Roast until potatoes are golden brown and barely tender, about 30 minutes. Cool to just warm.

While potatoes are roasting bring a large pot of salted water to boil. Add green beans and cook 5 minutes or just until crisp tender. Drain; rinse with cold water to stop the cooking process.

Place roasted potatoes and blanched green beans in a large bowl. Gently toss to combine.

In a small mixing bowl whisk together the dressing ingredients; pour over still warm potatoes and beans. Gently stir onion, celery and hard-boiled eggs into potato mixture. Cover and refrigerate several hours and up to overnight. Season to taste with salt and pepper.

To serve: Garnish with chopped fresh dill.

ROUGH-CUT COLE *Slaw* with Blue Cheese
[Serves 6]

prep time: 20 minutes

Make ahead: This tastes better made one day ahead. It keeps for a couple days in the fridge.

Tip: Stir in diced red onion or carrot if desired.

¼ cup white wine vinegar
⅓ cup olive oil
Pinch of cayenne pepper
2 tablespoons mayonnaise
1 head green cabbage, cored and coarsely sliced or shredded
½–¾ cup crumbled blue cheese, or to taste
¼ cup fresh parsley, finely chopped
Salt and generous amounts of black pepper to taste

In a large bowl, whisk together vinegar, olive oil, cayenne pepper and mayonnaise. Stir in the cabbage; mix thoroughly. Stir in blue cheese and parsley. Taste and season with salt and pepper. Cover and chill until ready to serve. Adjust seasonings again just before serving.

sides

with

style

MUSHROOM *Potatoes*
[Serves 6]

prep time: 20 minutes   **cook time:** 40 minutes

More food with a sense of humor! If you don't have nested cutters (though I highly recommend having a set—they have all kinds of uses) you can use an apple corer.

Make ahead: Potatoes can be cut several hours in advance. Place them in a large bowl covered with water: drain and pat dry before proceeding.

Tip: Roast the trimmings in a separate pan and turn them into hash browns in the morning.

2½ pounds red-skinned new potatoes, scrubbed and patted dry
3 tablespoons olive oil
Salt and pepper to taste
Garnish: chopped fresh parsley

Preheat oven to 400°F.

Insert a small (1-inch) round cutter into one end of a potato. With the cutter still in the potato, cut up to the cutter with a small sharp knife. Twist the knife around the potato. Remove the cutter and the piece of potato from the cutter end. You'll be left with a potato "mushroom" and the "o-shaped" piece of potato you've removed. Save the trimmings to use for another purpose, or discard.

On a rimmed baking sheet, toss prepared potatoes with olive oil. Season generously with salt and pepper. Roast until potatoes are golden brown and tender, about 40 minutes.

To serve: Transfer potatoes to a serving bowl or platter. Garnish with chopped parsley; serve.

GRILLED *Corn* with Roasted Garlic Butter

[Serves 6–8]

prep time: 20 minutes	*cook time:* 15 minutes

Make ahead: Roasted Garlic Butter can be made 2 days ahead. Cover and refrigerate until ready to use. Freeze, well-wrapped for a month.

Tip: Toss a slice or two of the Roasted Garlic Butter with freshly cooked pasta, place on grilled fish or shrimp or spread it on crusty bread.

ROASTED GARLIC BUTTER

2 large heads garlic, roasted (recipe follows)
1 tablespoon finely minced fresh chives
2 tablespoons finely minced roasted red pepper
1¼ sticks butter (10 tablespoons), softened
Salt and pepper to taste
2 tablespoons olive oil

In a medium mixing bowl, mash roasted garlic with a fork; stir in chives, roasted red pepper and butter. Season with salt and pepper. Place on a sheet of waxed paper and roll into a cylinder. Freeze or refrigerate until ready to use. Slice into "coins" to serve.

GRILLED CORN

6–8 ears fresh sweet corn, husked

Brush corn lightly with olive oil. Grill, turning occasionally, about 15 minutes or until corn is lightly browned in spots.

To serve: Serve hot, with Roasted Garlic Butter.

To roast garlic: Preheat oven to 350°F. Cut off and discard top quarter of each garlic head. Place garlic in small baking dish. Drizzle with 2 tablespoons oil. Cover dish with foil and bake until garlic is tender, about 1 hour 10 minutes. Cool garlic slightly. Squeeze garlic out of skins.

soups, salads & sides

ear

to

ear

CREAMED *Spinach*
[Serves 4]

prep time: 10 minutes   **cook time:** 10–12 minutes

Make ahead: Best made last minute but can be made a day ahead and gently reheated.

Tip: You can substitute a 10-ounce box of frozen chopped spinach for fresh. Skip the 2 minute cook time, just thaw and squeeze dry before adding to the sautéed shallot and onions.

2 pounds fresh spinach, stems removed
2 tablespoons unsalted butter
½ cup finely chopped shallots
1 teaspoon minced garlic
½ cup heavy cream
¾ teaspoon salt
½ teaspoon black pepper
¼ teaspoon nutmeg

Cook spinach for 2 minutes in a pot of boiling salted water; drain, pressing to remove as much water as possible. Set aside. Melt butter in a sauté pan over medium-high heat. Add the shallots and garlic. Cook, stirring, until soft, about 2 minutes. Add the spinach. Stir in the cream, salt, pepper, and nutmeg. Cook about 4 minutes; serve immediately.

SEASONED *Onion* STRAWS

[Serves 4]

prep time: 10 minutes

cook time: about 2 minutes per batch

Make ahead: These need to be made last minute, but if you pull all your prep together in advance they go together quickly.

Tip: A sweet onion, like a Vidalia, makes a really mellow and delicious onion straw.

Vegetable oil, as needed for frying
1 large sweet onion, peeled, halved and sliced into ¼-inch slices
¼ cup milk
½ teaspoon hot sauce
1 cup flour
1 teaspoon salt
½ teaspoon pepper
¼ teaspoon cayenne pepper
Salt and pepper to taste

Preheat oven to 200°F. In a deep heavy skillet or Dutch oven pour oil to the depth of 2-inches. Heat until very hot but not smoking.

In a medium bowl combine the sliced onion, milk and hot sauce. In a shallow dish combine the flour, salt, pepper and cayenne pepper. Working in batches, dip a few onion slices into the milk then dredge them in the seasoned flour. Fry until golden brown and crisp. Drain on paper towels; transfer to a paper towel lined baking sheet. Place in the oven while cooking remaining onion slices. Season with salt and pepper; serve immediately.

Color: When choosing a menu, include contrasting colors and use herbs, seasonings and simple sauces to accent flavor and bring color contrast.

Texture: Crispy, crunchy, creamy—combine elements for exciting texture. Many foods benefit from a sprinkle of chopped nuts, herbs or vegetables, but make sure the garnish "belongs" to the dish. A sprig of rosemary on lamb makes perfect sense, as do lemon slices on fish.

Shape: Think of the plate as picture frame and present food artfully inside it. Don't overcrowd—try to leave some empty spaces. Odd numbers are more appealing than even. Meats are more interesting when sliced and fanned out while sauces can create a feeling of shape and movement.

Simplicity: As a rule of thumb, the more complicated the dish, the simpler the garnish. Sometime the best garnish is minimal—or none at all.

Height: For interest, pack rice or mashed potatoes into ramekins and unmold it on the plate. Lean sliced steak or asparagus spears against it for variations in height. Top with a fresh herb sprig and see new excitement at your dinner table.

Beautiful plate presentation creates a sense of excitement and expectation, creating balance and contrast without overwhelming the food. A great looking plate combines color, texture, shape, simplicity and height.

entrées

OPEN FACED RATATOUILLE SANDWICHES with Gruyere — 64

STUFFED ITALIAN SANDWICH — 66

SALMON IN PHYLLO with Lemon and Herbs — 68

SEAFOOD STEW — 70

CREOLE PASTA — 72

BAKED MACARONI AND CHEESE with Buttered Crumb Topping — 74

CHICKEN AND BLACK BEAN ENCHILADAS
with Rose's Green Salsa and Guacamole — 76

ROSE'S GREEN SALSA and Guacamole — 78

CHICKEN PICCATTA — 80

MACADAMIA CHICKEN with Mango Butter Sauce — 82

BBQ CHICKEN PIZZA — 84

ASIAN BBQ RIBS — 86

BEEF TENDERLOIN with Horseradish Sauce — 88

BEEF TENDERLOIN STEW — 90

BEEF FAJITAS with Peppers and Onions — 92

CHILI with Sausage and Beef — 94

MUSTARD PORK TENDERLOIN with Cherry Cabernet Sauce — 96

OPEN FACED *Ratatouille* SANDWICHES with Gruyere
[Serves 6–8 as a side dish]

prep time: 20 minutes	*cook time:* 30 minutes	*wine suggestion:* Picpul

As a kid, when my Mom made ratatouille I'd suffer through it the first night, but I genuinely looked forward to when she served it, leftover, as an open-faced sandwich topped with melted cheese. It makes a great lunch or light dinner.

Baguettes, split
Ratatouille, recipe follows
Thinly sliced Gruyere cheese to taste

Preheat broiler. Mound the ratatouille on each half of the split baguettes. Top with thinly sliced Gruyere. Broil until bubbly and brown. Serve.

RATATOUILLE

Make ahead: Can be made several days ahead; refrigerate until ready to serve.

Tip: Try leftover Ratatouille in an omelet, sprinkled with Feta cheese.

Up to ½ cup olive oil, as needed
1 eggplant, peeled if desired, diced
1 zucchini, diced
1 summer squash, diced
1 red bell pepper, seeded and diced
1 red onion, finely chopped
3 tomatoes, roughly chopped
2 cloves garlic, minced
3 tablespoons finely chopped parsley
2 tablespoons finely chopped fresh basil
1 tablespoon finely chopped fresh thyme
Salt and pepper to taste

In a large Dutch oven or heavy pot, heat about 2 tablespoons olive oil over medium heat. Add eggplant; cook, stirring, until tender. Add a bit more oil to the pan; add zucchini, summer squash and onion; sauté 5 minutes. Add peppers and more oil as needed. Stir in chopped tomatoes, garlic and herbs; season with salt and pepper to taste. Simmer 15 minutes, or until mixture is heated through. Season with salt and pepper.

To serve: Serve warm, room temperature or chilled.

entrées

STUFFED *Italian* SANDWICH
[Serves 6–8 as a side dish]

prep time: 25 minutes	*chill time:* Overnight	*wine suggestion:* Italian Barbera

Make ahead: Must be made a day ahead; refrigerate. Let come to room temperature before serving.

Tip: Press the sandwich firmly and wrap it tightly for best results. Use your favorite meats and cheeses.

½ cup pesto, purchased or homemade
1 round (2-pound) loaf French or Italian bread
¼ pound thinly sliced salami
¼ pound thinly sliced pepperoni
¼ pound thinly sliced mortadella (or use any combination of your favorite Italian meats)
½ pound thinly sliced provolone
1 8-ounce jar roasted red peppers, drained
½ cup sliced black olives
½ sweet onion, very thinly sliced
2–3 plum tomatoes, thinly sliced

Cut bread in half horizontally. Remove enough of the soft inside to leave a 1-inch shell. Spread half the pesto inside the bottom. Layer with half the meat, cheese, peppers, olives, onions and tomatoes. Repeat with remaining meat, cheese, peppers, olives, onions and tomatoes. Spread the remaining pesto over the inside of the top of the bread shell. Press firmly onto filling. Wrap tightly in plastic wrap and refrigerate overnight.

To serve: Cut into slices.

entrées

SALMON IN *Phyllo* with Lemon and Herbs
[Serves 4]

| prep time: 10 minutes | bake time: 25–30 minutes | wine suggestion: Grenache |

This is a really nice way to serve fish. Adding flavorings between the layers of dough elevates it to a whole new level. This is great with a simple salad and steamed asparagus. In season, serve Peaches in Wine for dessert.

Make-ahead: Can be assembled early in the day and refrigerated until ready to bake.

Tip: The key to success with phyllo (or filo) is to keep it covered and work quickly. Gently unfold the thawed dough; cover with plastic wrap and then a damp kitchen towel. Every time you remove a sheet, re-cover the remaining dough immediately or it will dry out and crumble. You can re-freeze any unused dough, just be sure to wrap it well. For assembly, brush butter on the edges first, then work your way into the center.

4 sheets phyllo dough, thawed
¼ cup butter, melted
1 tablespoon minced fresh dill (or 1 teaspoon dried)
1 teaspoon lemon zest
Salt and pepper to taste
4 4-ounce salmon filets
Salt and pepper to taste
1 5.2-ounce box Boursin cheese

Preheat oven to 350°F . Spray a baking sheet with no-stick spray; set aside.

Lay one sheet of phyllo pastry on a work surface; brush with melted butter. Sprinkle evenly with a little minced dill and lemon zest. Top with a second sheet; brush with butter, sprinkle with dill and lemon zest. Repeat with third sheet and remaining dill and lemon zest. Top with fourth sheet; butter. Cut stacked dough into 4 equal rectangles. Generously season salmon with salt and pepper. Place seasoned salmon off-center along one long side of a dough rectangle. Top fish with slices (which will crumble) of Boursin cheese. Fold sides of dough over salmon; wrap and roll pastry to fully encase the fish and cheese. Brush with melted butter. Place seam side down on the prepared baking sheet. Bake 25–30 minutes or until golden brown. Let stand 5 or 6 minutes before serving.

entrées

SEAFOOD *Stew*

[Serves 6]

prep time: 20 minutes | **cook time:** 40 minutes | **wine suggestion:** Spanish Albarino

Make ahead: Stew can be made, up to the point of adding the seafood, one day ahead. Gently re-heat and add seafood as directed.

Tip: To chiffonade the basil, stack the leaves and roll them up like a cigar. Slice, across the roll, into thin strips.

3 tablespoons olive oil
1 onion, chopped
3 cloves garlic, minced
4 red skin potatoes, diced
1 each red and yellow bell peppers, seeded and chopped
1 zucchini, chopped
1 cup white wine
1 8-ounce bottle clam juice
1 28-ounce can diced tomatoes
1 bay leaf
1 pound sea bass (or any other firm mild fish) cut into 2-inch chunks
18 large shrimp, peeled and de-veined
12 sea scallops
½ cup fresh basil; cut into chiffonade
Salt and pepper
Hot sauce to taste
Garnish: Sliced green onions
Variation: You can also serve Seafood Stew in soup bowls over hot cooked rice for an even heartier meal

In a large Dutch oven, heat oil over medium high heat. Add onion, garlic and potatoes; sauté until tender, about 8 minutes. Add bell peppers; sauté 3–4 minutes. Add zucchini, wine, clam juice, tomatoes and bay leaf. Bring to a boil; reduce heat and simmer 15 minutes. Add fish, shrimp and scallops; simmer 5 minutes. Stir in basil. Season with salt, pepper and hot sauce to taste.

To serve: Garnish with green onions.

CREOLE *Pasta*

[Serves 4–6]

prep time: 20 minutes	*cook time:* 30 minutes	*wine suggestion:* Grenache

This colorful pasta dish is another favorite of my kid's. What's not to like? Shrimp, chicken, and sausage—it's got something for everyone. Serve with Parmesan cheese for sprinkling.

Make ahead: No

Tip: Warmed plates make a big difference when serving pasta. Warm them in a low oven or in a sink of very hot water.

1 pound fettuccine
¼ cup olive oil
2 tablespoons butter
1 small red onion, sliced into ¼" strips
2 cloves garlic, minced
1 red, yellow or orange pepper, seeded and sliced into ¼" strips
2 sun-dried tomato, minced
1 roasted red pepper from a jar, minced
2 cups cooked chicken, cut into ½" strips
12 large shrimp, uncooked, peeled & de-veined
2 cups andouille sausage, sliced into ¼" slices
2 teaspoons Cajun seasoning
1 pound fresh spinach, stems removed
1 cup cherry tomatoes, cut in half
Salt and pepper, to taste
Grated Parmesan cheese as an accompaniment

Bring a large pot of salted water to a boil. Cook fettuccine according to package directions.

Meanwhile, heat olive oil and butter in large sauté pan; add onion, garlic, bell peppers, sun-dried tomato, and roasted red pepper. Sauté until onion is beginning to soften, about 5 minutes.

Add remaining ingredients, except fettuccine, and sauté until thoroughly heated, about 6 minutes. Add cooked and drained fettuccine; season with salt and pepper. Toss well.

To serve: Transfer to warmed plates; serve with Parmesan cheese for topping.

entrées

BAKED *Macaroni* AND CHEESE with Buttered Crumb Topping

[Serves 4–6]

prep time: **10 minutes**   *cook time:* **30 minutes**

Make ahead: Bake and cool; refrigerate until ready to use. Reheat in low oven.

Tip: Mac and Cheese is always a favorite of kids—my son Sean and daughter Katie absolutely love this for dinner. The recipe changes based on what bits of cheese are in my fridge—so I encourage you to go beyond, way beyond Cheddar! And you can always toss in chopped ham, diced tomatoes or green chiles, too.

8 ounces macaroni or other tubular pasta
3 tablespoons butter
3 tablespoons flour
¼ teaspoon onion powder
1⅔ cups milk
2–3 cups shredded Cheddar cheese (or a mixture of Cheddar, Gouda, Fontina, Havarti, Mozzarella, etc)
Pinch cayenne pepper
1 tablespoon yellow mustard, plus more to taste
Salt and pepper to taste

TOPPING

1 tablespoon butter, melted
½ cup fine dry bread crumbs
Parmesan cheese

Preheat oven to 350°F. Spray a 2-quart casserole with cooking spray; set aside.

Cook macaroni as directed on package; drain. Transfer to prepared casserole; set aside.

While macaroni is cooking, melt butter in a medium saucepan. Stir in flour and onion powder; cook for about 1 minute. Gradually whisk in milk. Cook and stir over medium heat until mixture thickens and bubbles. Stir in cheese until smooth. Stir in a pinch of cayenne pepper. Generously season to taste with yellow mustard, salt and pepper. Add more cheese or mustard as needed. Remove from heat. Stir cheese sauce into macaroni.

Topping: In a small bowl combine melted butter and breadcrumbs. Sprinkle over macaroni and cheese. Sprinkle with a little freshly grated Parmesan cheese. Bake 25 minutes, or until bubbly and lightly browned on top. Let stand 5–10 minutes before serving.

CHICKEN AND BLACK BEAN *Enchiladas*
with Rose's Green Salsa and Guacamole [Serves 4–6]

| *prep time:* 30 minutes | *bake time:* 15–20 minutes | *wine suggestion:* Spanish Grenache or Mexican Beere |

Make ahead: Sauce and filling can be made a day ahead. Assemble within an hour or two of baking; refrigerate until ready to bake.

Tip: Keep cooked chicken in the freezer. Buy large packages of chicken breasts and grill or bake them and then shred, chop and slice it before dividing into meal-size packages. Freeze for a real time saver for future meals. You can replace the chicken in the Enchiladas with sliced steak, ground beef or shredded pork. If you're in a hurry, use purchased enchilada sauce.

ENCHILADA SAUCE
[Makes 2½ cups]

2 tablespoons vegetable oil
2 tablespoons flour
2 tablespoons chili powder
1½ teaspoons ground cumin
1 (8-ounce) can tomato sauce
1 (14-ounce) can chicken broth
1 teaspoon salt
¼ teaspoon garlic powder

Heat oil in a medium saucepan; stir in flour and chili powder. Cook for 1 minute. Add remaining ingredients bring to a boil; simmer about 10 minutes.

ENCHILADAS [See page 77 for directions]

2½ cups Enchilada Sauce, divided
2 cups shredded cooked chicken
1 cup black beans, rinsed and drained
3–4 green onions, thinly sliced
½ cup shredded Cheddar, divided
½ cup shredded Monterey Jack, divided
¼ cup sour cream plus more for garnish
1 4-ounce can diced green chiles
¼ cup chopped fresh cilantro, plus more for garnish
Salt and pepper, to taste
14 flour tortillas, 6-inch size

TOPPING

½ cup shredded Cheddar
½ cup Monterey Jack

entrées

Preheat oven to 350°F.

In a medium bowl, mix together the chicken, black beans, green onions, cheddar and Monterey Jack cheese, sour cream, chiles and cilantro. Stir in ½ cup of Enchilada sauce; stir until well blended. Season to taste with salt and pepper. Set aside.

Spray a 9x13 inch baking dish with cooking spray. Pour a small amount of Enchilada sauce over the bottom of the pan to lightly coat. Spread 2 heaping spoonfuls of the chicken mixture just off center of each tortilla and roll into loose cylinders. Place the enchiladas, seam side down, side by side in the prepared dish. Pour remaining sauce over, top with cheeses. Bake until bubbling and lightly browned, 15-20 minutes.

To serve: garnish with sour cream, sliced green onions and chopped cilantro

Salsa and Guacamole on page 78

ROSE'S GREEN *Salsa*

[Serves 8]

prep time: 5 minutes

Rose Grace is a dynamic woman who taught me a lot about the foods of her Mexican heritage. This simple salsa is made with tomatillos, which look like little green tomatoes in husks.

Make ahead: Can be made several days ahead; store in the refrigerator.

Tip: Start with one Serrano, add more if you want more heat.

1 pound tomatillos, husked, washed and roughly chopped
½ small onion, roughly chopped
1 medium bunch cilantro, stemmed, washed and chopped
1 Serrano chile (or more, to taste), stemmed and chopped
1 tablespoon olive oil
Salt and pepper to taste

Add chopped tomatillos, onion, cilantro and chilies to blender or food processor and pulse to create a rough puree. Season with salt and pepper. Serve with tortilla chips.

CHUNKY GUACAMOLE

[Serves 4–6]

prep time: 10 minutes

Make ahead: Can be made several hours in advance; refrigerate until ready to serve.

Tip: Press plastic wrap directly on the surface of the guacamole; refrigerate until ready to serve. The lime juice keeps it from discoloring.

2 ripe avocados, pitted and diced
½–1 cup sweet onion, finely diced
1 jalapeno pepper, seeded and minced
1 small tomato, seeded and chopped
Juice of 1 lime, or to taste
1–2 tablespoons finely minced fresh cilantro
Salt, to taste

In a medium bowl, lightly mix all ingredients until well blended. Taste and adjust seasonings with salt and hot sauce. Refrigerate, tightly covered, until ready to serve.

CHICKEN *Piccatta*

[Serves 4]

prep time: 20 minutes	cook time: 20 minutes	wine suggestion: Soave or Pinot Grigio

Serve with greens tossed with a lemony vinaigrette and orzo tossed with butter, parsley and Parmesan.

Make ahead: No

Tip: Buy extra chicken and pound it thin all at once. Freeze already pounded chicken breasts to make this dish even easier next time.

4 skinless boneless chicken breast halves
Salt and pepper to taste
1 cup flour
2 tablespoons olive oil, divided
⅓ cup dry white wine
¼ cup fresh lemon juice
¼ cup chicken broth, plus more as needed
1 tablespoon butter mixed with 1½ tablespoons flour
¼ cup capers, drained
¼ cup chopped fresh parsley
2 tablespoons butter, at room temperature

Place chicken between 2 large sheets of plastic wrap. Using the smooth side of a meat pounder or rolling pin, lightly pound chicken to ¼-inch thickness. Season both sides of chicken with salt and pepper. Place flour in shallow baking dish. Dip chicken into flour to coat; shake off excess.

Heat 1 tablespoon oil in heavy large skillet over medium high heat. Add 2 chicken breasts; cook until golden and cooked through, about 3 minutes per side. Repeat with remaining chicken and oil. Transfer chicken to platter; tent with foil to keep warm.

In the same skillet bring wine, lemon juice and broth to boil over medium-high heat. Whisk in butter-flour mixture; boil until sauce thickens slightly, about 2 minutes. Stir in capers, parsley and butter. Season sauce to taste with salt and pepper. Thin with broth if needed.

To serve: Pour sauce over chicken; serve.

entrées

MACADAMIA *Chicken* with Mango Butter Sauce

[Serves 4]

prep time: 20 minutes	cook time: 30 minutes	wine suggestion: Chardonnay

Make ahead: Chicken breast halves can be coated; refrigerate until ready to cook. Add a minute or two to the cook time for chilled chicken. The sauce can be made an hour ahead and held in a thermos to keep warm.

MANGO BUTTER SAUCE

2 shallots, minced
1 cup dry white wine
½ cup diced ripe mango
1 teaspoon whole peppercorns
1 tablespoon whole coriander
¾ cup (1½ sticks) unsalted butter, sliced into pats
10 mint leaves, finely minced
Salt and white pepper, to taste

In a small saucepan over medium heat combine the shallots, wine, diced mango, peppercorns and coriander; simmer until less than half the liquid remains. Strain out the solids, pressing with a spoon. Return the strained liquid to the pan; discard the solids. Bring the liquid back to a simmer; whisk in the butter, one pat at a time, until completely incorporated. Remove from heat; stir in the mint, salt and pepper. Keep warm until ready to serve.

MACADAMIA CHICKEN

4 skinless, boneless chicken breast halves
Salt and pepper, to taste
1 cup flour
3 eggs, beaten
½ cup finely ground macadamia nuts
1 cup panko bread crumbs
1 tablespoon butter, plus more as needed
1 tablespoon olive oil, plus more as needed

Garnish: Diced mango and mint sprigs

Season both sides of the chicken with salt and pepper. Place the flour in a shallow dish. Place the eggs in another shallow dish. In a third shallow dish combine the macadamia nuts and panko breadcrumbs. Lightly coat each chicken breast half with flour, shaking off any excess. Dip in egg, and coat with the macadamia nut mixture. In a large sauté pan heat the butter and olive oil over medium heat. Sauté the chicken until browned, about 5 minutes per side.

To serve: Top each chicken breast with Mango Butter Sauce; garnish with diced mango and a sprig of mint.

BBQ *Chicken* PIZZA

[Serves 4]

| *prep time:* 10 minutes | *cook time:* 10–12 minutes | *wine suggestion:* Zinfandel |

Make ahead: No

Tip: See the tip on pre-cooking chicken from the Chicken and Black Bean Enchilada recipe to make this pizza go together quickly.

1½ cups cooked chicken breast, shredded or cut into ¼-inch slices
1 tablespoon olive oil
1 medium onion, peeled and thinly sliced
1 cup thinly sliced mushrooms
1 red pepper, seeded and sliced into strips
1 cup frozen corn
½ cup barbecue sauce
1 12-inch pre-baked pizza crust
1 cup grated smoked Gouda
1 cup shredded mozzarella cheese

Preheat oven to 450°F.

Heat oil in large skillet over medium-high heat. Add onion, mushrooms and red pepper to pan; sauté 3 minutes, or until onion is translucent. Remove pan from heat. Stir in chicken, corn and barbecue sauce.

Place pizza crust on baking sheet. Sprinkle half the cheese on pizza crust. Top with chicken mixture. Top with remaining cheese. Bake 10–12 minutes, or until crust is crisp and cheese melts.

Let stand 3 minutes before cutting. Serve immediately.

entrées

ASIAN BBQ *Ribs*
[Serves 4–6]

prep time: 20 minutes	cook time: 2 hours	wine suggestion: Syrah or Malbec

Make ahead: Sauce can be made several days ahead; refrigerate until ready to serve. Ribs can be baked a day ahead; refrigerate until ready to finish on the grill.

Tip: The sugar in BBQ sauce can burn quickly so always sauce during the last minutes of grilling. Try this sauce on chicken, too.

SAUCE

2 cloves garlic, minced
1 tablespoon dry mustard
1 tablespoon crushed red pepper flakes
1 tablespoon fresh ginger, minced
1 small onion, finely chopped
1 cup brown sugar, packed
¼ cup soy sauce
¾ cup rice vinegar
1 cup crushed tomatoes
2 cups hoisin sauce

3 finely sliced green onions
½ cup chopped cilantro

4 racks baby back ribs
Salt and pepper to taste
1 cup water

In a medium saucepan combine the sauce ingredients; simmer for about an hour.

Add the green onions and cilantro; simmer a few minutes more. Remove from heat; cool slightly. Use a stick blender or transfer to a blender or food processor; puree until smooth.

Preheat oven to 350°F. Season the ribs with salt and pepper. Place in a single layer in a roasting pan; add 1 cup water. Cover pan with foil. Bake 1½ hours.
Grill the ribs over medium-hot grill until heated through, about 3 minutes per side. Baste with BBQ sauce on both sides while grilling.

To serve: Transfer to a serving platter; serve with additional BBQ sauce.

grills

gone

wild

BEEF *Tenderloin* with Horseradish Sauce

[Serves 6]

prep time: 10 minutes	cook time: 40 minutes	wine suggestion: Pinot Noir

Beef tenderloin is a dinner party staple for me. While it is expensive, it's pretty fool proof and always delicious. Serve it with either the Horseradish Cream Sauce or the Blue Cheese butter. Mushroom Potatoes and Creamed Spinach are nice accompaniments. Go all the way and serve Creamy Cheesecake for dessert.

Make ahead: Tenderloin can be seared ahead. Refrigerate. Just before roasting, bring back to room temperature before proceeding as directed.

Tip: Bring the meat to room temperature before cooking. Start in a very hot oven; immediately reduce the heat. There will be carry over cooking, so take it out before it's reached the done-ness you want. Always let it rest before carving, allowing the juices to settle back into the meat.

One 4-pound beef tenderloin, trimmed
Olive oil
Salt and pepper
1 tablespoon Dijon mustard

Preheat oven to 500°F. Rub the tenderloin with olive oil; season generously with salt and pepper. Heat oil in large, heavy skillet over high heat. Add beef; sear until brown on all sides, about 5 minutes total. Transfer beef to a rimmed baking sheet. Rub all over with 1 tablespoon Dijon mustard. Place in oven; immediately reduce heat to 350°F. To end up with perfectly medium rare beef, roast until thermometer inserted into center of beef registers 120–125°F, about 35 minutes. Transfer beef to cutting board; tent with foil and let rest 10 minutes before slicing.

To serve: Slice and serve with Horseradish Cream Sauce or Blue Cheese Butter.

Sauce on page 89

entrées

HORSERADISH CREAM SAUCE
[Makes about 1½ cups]

1 cup sour cream
⅓ cup prepared horseradish (not horseradish
    sauce)
2 teaspoons Dijon mustard
1 tablespoon finely minced shallot
1 tablespoon finely minced fresh chives
1 teaspoon lemon juice
Heavy cream as needed
Salt and pepper to taste

In a medium mixing bowl whisk together all sauce
ingredients. Taste; season with salt and pepper. Thin
with a little heavy cream if needed. Chill until ready
to serve.

BLUE CHEESE BUTTER
[Makes about ½ cup]

Make ahead: Compound butters freeze beautifully. Wrap securely in plastic wrap then a Ziploc.
Slice off pieces as needed. Serve with meats, fish,
breads or use to flavor rice, vegetables or sauces.

1 stick unsalted butter, at room temperature
¼ cup crumbled blue cheese, at room temperature
2 green onions, thinly sliced
1 teaspoon cracked black pepper

In a medium mixing bowl combine all the
ingredients. Transfer mixture to the center
of a piece of parchment paper or plastic wrap.
Fold one edge of the paper over the butter. Roll
back and forth to create a log shape. Twist the
ends of the paper; refrigerate until firm. Slice
into coins. Top slices of beef tenderloin or
grilled steak with a coin of butter.

BEEF TENDERLOIN *Stew*

[Serves 4–6]

prep time: 20 minutes	*cook time:* 1 hour 45 minutes	*wine suggestion:* Syrah

Make ahead: Can be made 1 day in advance and re-heated over gentle heat.

Tip: Beef Tenderloin Stew is a totally decadent "leftover" to make with trimmings from tenderloin roasted for another purpose. I usually buy about an extra pound and get the other half pound from trimmings.

1½ cups flour mixed with generous salt and pepper, to taste
6–8 tablespoons olive oil, divided
1½ pounds beef tenderloin, cut into 1-inch cubes
6 shallots, finely diced
1 large onion, diced
2 tablespoons tomato paste
1–1½ cups dry red wine
2 (14.5-ounce) cans beef broth
3 medium potatoes, peeled and cut into 2-inch cubes
3 carrots, peeled and cut into 2-inch pieces
3 ribs celery, cut into 2-inch pieces
8 ounces mushrooms, stemmed, and quartered
1 tablespoon chopped fresh marjoram or 1 teaspoon dried

Place flour in shallow dish; season with salt and pepper. In large heavy Dutch oven over medium-high heat, heat about 2 tablespoons olive oil. Working in batches, coat beef with flour; add to pot and brown on all sides. Using slotted spoon, transfer to plate. Add more olive oil as needed with each batch.

Add 2 more tablespoons olive oil to the same pot over medium-high heat. Add shallots and onions; sauté until tender, about 6 minutes. Mix in tomato paste, then wine. Bring to boil, scraping up any browned bits. Add broth, then beef and any juices from the plate. Bring to boil. Reduce heat, cover partially and simmer about 10 minutes.

Add potatoes, carrots and celery; simmer uncovered until vegetables are just tender, about an hour. Add mushrooms and marjoram; simmer until mushrooms are tender, about 5 minutes. Season with salt and pepper. Serve.

BEEF *Fajitas* with Peppers and Onions
[Serves 4–6]

prep time: 30 minutes	*cook time:* 25 minutes	*wine suggestion:* Malbec

Make ahead: No

Tip: You can replace the beef with grilled chicken or fish.

1½–2 pounds flank steak
½ cup olive oil
Juice of 2 limes
1 teaspoon salt
¼ cup cracked black pepper

PEPPERS AND ONIONS

⅓ cup olive oil
1 tablespoon balsamic vinegar
2–3 medium onions, peeled, cut into 6 wedges, root ends intact
2 red, orange or yellow bell peppers, seeded and cut into strips
Salt and pepper to taste

12 flour tortillas

Garnish: Sour Cream, Guacamole

Heat grill. Soak 4–6 wooden skewers in water.

In a shallow dish combine the olive oil, lime juice and salt. Add the flank steak. Let marinate at room temperature while preparing the rest of the meal, turning occasionally. When ready to grill, remove steak from the marinade; discard marinade. Season both sides with salt and the ¼ cup cracked black pepper.

In a medium mixing bowl combine the olive oil and balsamic vinegar. Add the onions and bell pepper strips; toss to coat. Let stand at room temperature. When ready to grill thread onions and peppers onto soaked skewers. Season with salt and pepper.

Place onion and pepper skewers on the grill. Grill, turning occasionally, for about 10 minutes before adding the steak to the grill. Continue to grill, turning steak only once, about 10 minutes for medium rare. Transfer vegetables to a platter; cover with foil to keep warm. Transfer steak to a cutting board; let stand 5 minutes before slicing across the grain into thin slices.

While the steak is resting, place the tortillas directly on the grill rack, turning once, until puffed and slightly brown in spots, about 1 minute.

To serve: Serve steak, onions and peppers with sour cream and guacamole and the toasted tortillas.

make

it

sizzle

Chili with Sausage and Beef

[Serves 8]

prep time: 20 minutes   **cook time:** about an hour   **wine suggestion:** Syrah or Zinfandel

Make ahead: Can be made a day or two ahead. Cool before refrigerating, and then reheat just before serving.

Tip: Adjust the spices to your taste—this recipe is a starting point for a nice medium chili. If you can find "fire roasted" tomatoes, try them—they add a nice, smoky flavor.

1 pound ground beef or turkey
1 pound hot Italian sausage, casings removed
3 tablespoons olive oil
2 medium onions, chopped
1 red bell pepper, seeded and chopped
1–2 jalapeno peppers, seeded and minced
3 cloves garlic, minced
3 tablespoons chili powder
1 tablespoon oregano
1 bay leaf
2 tablespoons ground cumin
1 14.5 ounce can diced tomatoes
1 14.5 ounce can crushed tomatoes
1 14.5 ounce can beef broth
1 (14.5-ounce) can black beans, rinsed and drained
1 (14.5-ounce) can kidney beans, rinsed and drained
Salt and pepper to taste

Garnish: Sour cream, shredded Monterey Jack, tortilla chips

In a large heavy pot over medium-high heat combine ground beef and sausage; crumble and cook until browned, about 10 minutes. Drain; reserve meat mixture and set aside. In the same pot heat olive oil over medium high heat; add onions, red bell pepper, jalapeno pepper and garlic; sauté until onions are tender, about 6 minutes. Stir in chili powder, oregano, bay leaf and cumin; cook about 1 minute or until fragrant. Stir in tomatoes and beef broth; bring to a boil. Reduce heat; stir in reserved meat mixture. Simmer 20 minutes, stirring occasionally. Stir in beans; simmer 15 minutes more. Season with salt and pepper.

To serve: Serve with sour cream, shredded cheese and tortilla chips.

MUSTARD *Pork* TENDERLOIN with Cherry Cabernet Sauce
[Serves 4]

| prep time: 10 minutes | cook time: 8–10 minutes | wine suggestion: Cotes du Rhone Rouge |

Marinate time: at least 4 hours and up to overnight

Make ahead: Tenderloin can be marinated the day before. Cherry Cabernet Sauce can be made a day ahead; re-heat gently and whisk in the butter just before serving.

Tip: If you have any leftovers, it makes a great sandwich.

MARINADE

¼ cup olive oil
1 clove garlic, finely minced
¼ cup Dijon mustard
1 teaspoon black pepper
½ teaspoon fine sea salt
1 teaspoon finely chopped fresh thyme
1 teaspoon finely chopped fresh rosemary

1 pork tenderloin (about 1¼ pounds) trimmed

In a medium mixing bowl, stir together the marinade ingredients. Place tenderloin in a shallow dish; rub marinade over pork. Refrigerate 4 hours and up to overnight. Grill or broil tenderloin until medium, about 8–10 minutes. Let rest 10 minutes; slice on bias into ¼ inch slices.

Cherry Cabernet Sauce on page 97

entrées

CHERRY CABERNET SAUCE

prep time: 10 minutes | **cook time:** 20–25 minutes

Make ahead: Reduce sauce to syrupy stage; cool and refrigerate until needed. Bring to a boil; remove from heat and whisk in chilled butter. Serve.

1 tablespoon olive oil
½ small red onion, diced
¼ cup chopped mushrooms
3 cups beef broth
1 teaspoon orange zest
2 cups Cabernet Sauvignon
1 cup dried cherries
¼ cup orange juice
1 tablespoon finely chopped fresh thyme
½ cup Port
3 tablespoons chilled butter, cut into pieces

Heat olive oil in a medium saucepan; add onions and mushrooms. Sauté 5 minutes.
Add beef broth, orange zest and wine. Bring to a boil; continue cooking until liquid
is reduced by half. Add dried cherries, orange juice, thyme and port; return to a
boil and cook until liquid is syrupy. Remove from heat and whisk in chilled butter,
one piece at a time.

To serve: Top sliced pork with Cherry Cabernet Sauce; serve.

desserts

We don't eat dessert every night at our house, but I always make dessert for a dinner party or holiday meal. Since my approach to cooking and entertaining is a simple one, I choose which dessert to serve by balancing the effort required with the rest of my menu. A more complicated entrée gets a simpler dessert—and vice versa. All of my favorite desserts are make ahead.

LEMON PANNA COTTA with Berry Sauce ... 100

PEACHES IN WINE ... 102

FRUIT TART with Gingersnap Cookie Crust ... 104

CHERRY ALMOND APRICOT TART ... 106

ALMOND SHORTCAKES with Double Cream and Triple Berries ... 108

SPICED PUMPKIN PIE with Bourbon Cream ... 110

CARAMEL CREPES with Brandied Caramel Sauce and Toasted Pecans ... 112

BUTTERMILK BANANA CAKE with Cream Cheese Cloud Frosting ... 114

CREAMY CHEESECAKE ... 116

DOUBLE CHOCOLATE MOUSSE TART with Chocolate Cookie Crust ... 118

CHOCOLATE BOWLS and Raspberry Sauce ... 120

ICE BOWLS with Sorbet ... 122

LIMONCELLO ... 124

Lemon PANNA COTTA with Berry Sauce

[Serves 6]

prep time: 45 minutes | *chill time:* 6 hours to overnight

Make ahead: Both the Panna Cotta and the Berry Sauce can be made one day ahead. Store separately; top the Panna Cotta with Berry Sauce just before serving.

Tip: Use crème fraîche or sour cream with great results.

1 cup whole milk
1 cup heavy cream
1 teaspoon vanilla extract
1 lemon
5 tablespoons fresh lemon juice
1 envelope (2 teaspoons) unflavored gelatin
½ cup sugar
1 cup crème fraîche or sour cream

SAUCE

1 16-ounce bag frozen mixed berries, thawed, juices reserved
3 tablespoons brown sugar
3 tablespoons crème de cassis (black-currant liqueur), optional

Garnish: Assorted fresh berries, mint sprigs

PANNA COTTA

Place 6 martini or wine glasses on a tray; set aside.
In a heavy saucepan combine milk, cream and vanilla extract. Using a small sharp knife, remove the peel from the lemon in long strips; add peel to cream mixture. Bring to a simmer. Remove from heat; let stand for 30 minutes. Strain to remove lemon peel; return strained mixture to saucepan.

Pour lemon juice into small bowl; sprinkle gelatin over. Let stand until gelatin softens, about 10 minutes. Stir gelatin mixture into milk mixture. Stir in sugar. Cook and stir over low heat just until sugar and gelatin dissolve, about 2 minutes. Remove from heat. Whisk in crème fraîche. Divide among glasses. Cover; chill until set, at least 6 hours or overnight.

SAUCE

In a food processor or blender, puree the berries and juices, brown sugar, and crème de cassis. Pour mixture though a mesh sieve set over a medium bowl, pressing to extract as much liquid as possible. Discard solids in sieve.

Assembly: Just before serving, spoon a little Berry Sauce over each Panna Cotta. Garnish with a handful of fresh berries and a mint sprig.

PEACHES IN *Wine*
[Serves 4]

prep time: 10 minutes

This is the quintessential summer dinner party dessert. It's nearly effortless and uses no heat—and it tastes so good even the peaches are grateful! Make sure to use a wine that you'd drink and enjoy.

Make ahead: The peaches need to sit in the wine for several hours; let stand at room temperature until ready to serve.

Tip: Serve with Italian amaretti cookies.

1 bottle Pinot Noir or Zinfandel
3–4 ripe but firm peaches

Wash the peaches. Slice each into 8 wedges; place in a large glass bowl. Pour red wine over and let stand, covered, at room temperature for several hours and up to overnight.

To serve: Using a slotted spoon, remove peaches from the wine and transfer to 4 large wine glasses. Spoon a little wine over top.

make

it

simple

FRUIT *Tart* with Gingersnap Cookie Crust

[Makes 1 10-inch tart]

prep time: 30 minutes	bake time: 8 minutes

Make ahead: Tart must chill several hours and can be made 24 hours in advance; refrigerate until ready to garnish with fruit. Add fruit and glaze no more than a couple hours in advance.

Tip: Select a variety of fresh fruits and berries or use all one kind for a different look. Well-drained Mandarin oranges work better than fresh. Most any cookie works for this crust recipe—try graham crackers, sugar cookies, vanilla wafers or Oreos with your favorite tart filling.

CRUST

2 cups ground gingersnap cookies (about 38 cookies)
2 tablespoons sugar
1/3 cup butter, melted

FILLING

1 cup mascarpone cheese, at room temperature
1/4 cup sugar
2 teaspoons lemon juice
1/2 cup heavy cream

GARNISH

Assorted fruit: raspberries, strawberries, blueberries, kiwi, oranges, red or green grapes
1/4 cup apricot preserves, melted and strained

Preheat oven to 350°F. In the bowl of a food processor, combine cookies and sugar; pulse until fine crumbs are made. Add butter and pulse until moist clumps form. Press mixture into bottom and up sides of a 10-inch removable bottom tart pan. Bake until golden, about 8 minutes. Watch carefully as it can easily burn at the end of cooking time. Let cool.

In the bowl of an electric mixer, combine mascarpone, sugar and lemon juice; beat at medium speed until well blended. Add heavy cream; beat at high speed until light and fluffy. Spread in tart shell and chill several hours.

Assembly: Arrange fruit on top of chilled filling. Using a small soft pastry brush, gently brush melted preserves over top.

CHERRY ALMOND APRICOT *Tart*

[Makes 1 10-inch]

| **prep time:** 20 minutes | **chill time:** 30 minutes | **bake time:** 35–40 minutes |

Make ahead: Tart can be made early in the day; store at room temperature.

Tip: You can substitute canned apricots and cherries for fresh if desired.

CRUST

1½ cups flour
1½ tablespoons sugar
⅛ teaspoon salt
9 tablespoons cold unsalted butter, cut into small pieces
½ cup ice water, more as needed

FILLING

½ cup almond paste
¼ cup unsalted butter
1 tablespoon sugar
2 teaspoons flour
1 egg, beaten

TOPPING

2 pounds small apricots, halved and pitted
½ pound cherries, pitted
2 tablespoons sugar
2 tablespoons unsalted butter, melted
1 tablespoon sugar

Crust: Position oven rack in the lowest position. Preheat oven to 400°F. In the bowl of a food processor, combine the flour, sugar, and salt. Add the butter; pulse until butter is the size of small peas. Gradually add ice water while pulsing until dough begins to stick together, being careful not to over mix. Shape dough into a flat disc, wrap in plastic wrap and refrigerate at least 30 minutes. Roll out dough into a circle ¼-inch thick; fit into a 10-inch tart pan with a removable bottom. Place on a baking sheet. Refrigerate until ready to use.

Filling: In the bowl of a food processor or electric mixer, combine the almond paste and butter until light and fluffy. Add the sugar and flour; mix until thoroughly combined. Add the egg; mix until completely incorporated. Remove crust from the refrigerator; spread filling evenly over crust.

Fruit topping: Arrange apricots cut-side down over the filling; fill spaces with cherries. Sprinkle with sugar. Brush with melted butter; sprinkle with sugar. Bake until crust is golden, 35–40 minutes.

Serve: Warm or at room temperature.

ALMOND *Shortcakes* with Double Cream and Triple Berries
[Serves 8]

prep time: 30 minutes	bake time: 10 minutes

Make ahead: The Almond Shortcakes are best when served within hours of baking but can be baked and stored in an airtight container at room temperature 1 day ahead. The Double Cream can be whipped several hours in advance and refrigerated until ready to use.

Tip: Use your favorite berries tossed with brown sugar or try sliced peaches as a variation.

SHORTCAKES

1½ cups flour
¼ cup sugar
3½ teaspoons baking powder
¼ teaspoon salt
1 tablespoon finely minced lemon zest
1 cup heavy cream, plus more as needed
½ teaspoon vanilla extract
¼ cup finely ground almonds
¼ cup brown sugar

DOUBLE CREAM

1 cup heavy cream
¼ cup sugar
½ cup crème fraiche or sour cream

3 cups assorted berries (combination of sliced strawberries, raspberries and blueberries)
¼ cup brown sugar

Preheat oven to 375°F. In a medium mixing bowl, combine flour, sugar, baking powder, salt, and lemon zest; mix well. In an electric mixer with a whip attachment, whip cream with vanilla extract until soft peaks form. Using the paddle attachment, add the flour mixture to the cream and beat on low speed until the flour is well blended. Turn dough onto a lightly floured surface and knead lightly. Roll the dough into an 8-inch circle about ¾-inch thick. In a small bowl, combine the almonds and brown sugar. Brush the dough with a little cream and generously sprinkle with the almond-brown sugar mixture. Cut into 8 wedges. Transfer to a baking pan; bake until golden brown, about 10 minutes. Remove from oven and cool on a rack before removing from baking pan.

Double cream: Whip the heavy cream; gradually add sugar. Gently fold in crème fraiche. Toss the berries with brown sugar; let stand for 5 minutes.

To serve: Split shortcakes in half. Place the bottom halves on 8 dessert plates; top with berries, cream, and the tops. Serve.

is

best

SPICED PUMPKIN *Pie* with Bourbon Cream

[Makes 1 8-inch pie]

prep time: 25 minutes | **bake time: 40–45 minutes**

Make ahead: Can be made 2 days ahead and chilled until ready to serve. Bourbon Cream can be made several hours in advance and chilled until ready to serve.

Tip: I learned the idea of adding bourbon to whipped cream from Chef Richard Perry. I've served it with my pumpkin pie every Thanksgiving since. Try the Bourbon Cream with Pecan Pie, too.

1 9-inch unbaked pie shell
1 cup packed brown sugar
½ cup sugar
2 tablespoons flour
½ teaspoon salt
1 teaspoon ground cinnamon
½ teaspoon ground allspice
½ teaspoon ground cloves
½ teaspoon ground ginger
1½ cups canned solid pack pumpkin (not pie filling)
2 tablespoons molasses
3 large eggs
1 cup heavy cream

Preheat oven to 375°F. Set pastry shell aside.
In the bowl of an electric mixer combine the sugars, flour, salt and spices to blend. Add the pumpkin, molasses, eggs and cream. Mix just to combine. Pour mixture into crust. Bake 40–45 minutes until the filling is set in the center. Cool on a wire rack.

BOURBON CREAM

1 cup heavy cream
2 tablespoons sugar
1½ tablespoons Bourbon (or to taste)

In the bowl of an electric mixer, combine heavy cream, sugar and bourbon. Beat until soft peaks form. Chill until ready to serve.

To serve: Garnish each slice with a Pastry Leaf, Candy Acorn and Bourbon Cream.

PASTRY LEAF GARNISH

[Enough pastry for 1 9-inch pie]

Egg wash made with 1 egg mixed
with 1 teaspoon water
Food coloring
Small artist's paint brush

Preheat oven to 400°F.
Roll out pastry; cut with leaf-shaped cutters (or by
hand with a small, sharp knife)
Transfer cut-outs to a piece of parchment paper.

Divide egg wash into 3 small bowls. Add a drop or
two of yellow food coloring to one bowl, green to
another and red and yellow to the third. Stir each
to combine.

Brush each leaf cut-out with colored egg wash,
starting with the lightest color first. Overlap with
varying colors.

Transfer colored cut-outs to a baking sheet; bake
6–8 minutes or until golden brown.
Cool 10 minutes on the baking sheet, remove to
rack to cool completely.
Use to garnish a whole pie or pie slices.

CANDY ACORNS

1 cup chocolate chips
Pecan halves
Finely chopped nuts

Place the chocolate chips in a small microwave
safe bowl. Melt the chocolate at 50 percent
power for 1½ minutes. Stir until chocolate is
completely melted and smooth.

Spread a little melted chocolate onto one pecan
half, sandwich with the second half.
Dip the top ⅓ of nut into melted chocolate; roll in
finely chopped nuts.

CARAMEL *Crepes* with Brandied Caramel Sauce and Toasted Pecans

[Makes 1 10-inch]

| *prep time:* 10 minutes | *chill time:* 1 hour to overnight | *cook time:* about 2 minutes |

Make ahead: The crepes can be made ahead and refrigerated for several days or frozen for a month. Assemble and bake just before serving.

Tip: Crepes freeze beautifully. Stack them between sheets of waxed paper. Place the stacks in Ziploc bags. Thaw at room temperature.

CREPES

1¹/₃ cups whole milk, at room temperature
1 cup flour
3 eggs
3 tablespoons unsalted butter, melted
1 tablespoon sugar
1 teaspoon salt

In a blender or food processor, combine all ingredients. Process just until smooth.

Cover and chill at least an hour and up to overnight.

Spray a 7-inch non-stick skillet with cooking spray; heat over medium heat. Add 2 tablespoons batter; swirl to coat the pan. Cook about 1 minute. Turn and cook 30 seconds more. Transfer to a plate.
Continue with remaining batter.

CARAMEL SAUCE and Toppings

1 cup purchased caramel sauce
2 tablespoons Cognac or brandy
1 cup toasted pecans, roughly chopped
Vanilla ice cream as an accompaniment

In a medium saucepan combine caramel sauce and cognac; heat until warmed through and melted. Cool slightly

Preheat oven to 350°F. Fill one crepe with 1 tablespoon sauce and sprinkle with chopped pecans. Fold crepe in half over filling, then in half again, forming a triangle. Place in a 13x9 inch baking dish. Repeat with remaining crepes. Pour remaining sauce over crepes. Bake just until heated through, about 15 minutes.

To serve: Sprinkle with remaining pecans. Serve with vanilla ice cream if desired.

BUTTERMILK *Banana* CAKE with Cream Cheese Cloud Frosting

[Makes 1 9-inch layer cake]

prep time: 30 minutes | **bake time: 30–35 minutes**

Make ahead: Cake can be baked and frosted a day ahead; refrigerate until ready.
to serve.

Tip: Keep a cake mix in the cupboard and over-ripe bananas in the freezer, and then
you can whip up this cake whenever the mood strikes. The banana skins turn black in
the freezer but they work perfectly for this cake—or your favorite banana bread.
Try the frosting on carrot cake and spice cake, too.

1 18.25-ounce white or yellow cake mix
2 teaspoons ground cinnamon
2 ripe bananas, peeled and mashed
½ cup buttermilk
½ cup water
½ cup canola oil
3 large eggs
½ teaspoon banana extract (optional)
½ cup finely chopped pecans

Preheat oven to 350°F. Spray two 9-inch round cake pans with cooking spray;
set aside.

In the bowl of an electric mixer, combine cake mix with remaining ingredients; mix
on low speed for 1 minute. Increase speed to medium and beat 2 minutes or until
batter is well blended, scraping the sides of the bowl as needed. Divide batter between
prepared pans. Bake 30–35 minutes or until a toothpick inserted in the center comes
out clean. Cool on wire racks 10 minutes; remove from pans and cool completely.
Frost with Cream Cheese Cloud Frosting; refrigerate until ready to serve.
Refrigerate any leftovers.

CREAM CHEESE CLOUD FROSTING

[Frosts and fills 1 9-inch layer cake]

1 8-ounce package cream cheese, softened
½ cup butter, softened
1 teaspoon vanilla extract
2 cups confectioners' sugar
¾ cup heavy cream

Place softened cream cheese and butter in the bowl of an electric mixer; mix on medium high speed until well blended and light. Add vanilla extract. Turn the mixer to low
speed; gradually add confectioners' sugar, ¼ cup at a time, and mix until well incorporated. Increase speed to medium high; beat 2 minutes. Slowly add the heavy cream;
beat until light and fluffy. Use immediately to frost cake. Refrigerate any leftovers.

cut

the

cake

CREAMY *Cheesecake*

[Makes 1 10-inch cheesecake]

prep time: 30 minutes	*chill time:* overnight	*bake time:* 1 hour 15 minutes plus 1 hour stand in turned-off oven

My husband never liked cheesecake until Trina Liss, a talented cooking instructor with whom I had once catered, taught me how to make this one. Now it's his most frequent dessert request. It's remarkably smooth and creamy.

Make ahead: Absolutely must be made ahead. Freezes beautifully.

Tip: Make sure all ingredients are at room temperature before beginning this recipe. Low, slow baking with room temperature ingredients helps avoid cracking. I like to freeze the cheesecake and slice it, frozen, an hour or so before we sit down for dinner. The cake is thawed in time for dessert and you get the cleanest slices possible.

4 8-ounce packages cream cheese, at room temperature
2 cups sugar
4 eggs, at room temperature
2 cups sour cream, at room temperature
1 cup heavy cream, at room temperature
1 teaspoon vanilla extract
2 teaspoons lemon juice
2 tablespoons butter, melted and cooled to room temperature

Garnish: Raspberry Sauce or fruit puree, sliced fruit or berries and mint sprigs. See page 120 for Raspberry Sauce recipe.

Position oven racks to bottom and center positions. Place a roasting pan filled with water on the bottom rack. Preheat oven to 350°F. Butter the bottom and sides of a 10-inch spring form pan; set aside.

In the bowl of an electric mixer, fitted with the whisk attachment, beat cream cheese and sugar until very smooth, about 3 minutes. Add eggs, one at a time, beating well after each addition. Add remaining ingredients, beating just until incorporated. Pour batter into prepared pan.

Set cheesecake on the rack above the roasting pan filled with water. Bake for 1 hour and 15 minutes. Turn off oven, leaving door closed. Do not open oven door. Let cake sit in closed oven for 1 hour. Remove from oven; cool in the pan on a cooling rack. When completely cool, cover with plastic wrap and refrigerate overnight

To un-mold, run a sharp knife around the edge of the pan. Place a plastic wrapped tray over cake and invert. Remove the base, then re-invert.

To serve: Garnish with Raspberry Sauce or fruit puree, sliced fruit or berries and top with a sprig of mint.

DOUBLE CHOCOLATE MOUSSE *Tart* with Cookie Crust
[Makes 1 9-inch tart]

| *prep time:* 45 minutes | *chill time:* 6 hours to overnight | *bake time:* 5 minutes |

Chef Steve Hellmich is one of my favorite cooking teachers. He does wonderful desserts and he brought a variation on this one to me years ago. I've added an easy egg-less mousse filling for a really simple dessert that's always a hit.

Make ahead: Can be made one day in advance; chill until ready to garnish with whipped cream.

Tip: The Chocolate Mousse makes a great dessert on its own, served in wine glasses or the Chocolate Bowls. Try it as a cake filling, too.

CRUST

21 chocolate sandwich cookies
¼ cup (½ stick) unsalted butter, softened
Mousse:
12 ounces semisweet chocolate, finely chopped
1 teaspoon vanilla extract
Pinch of salt
1 cup heavy cream
2 cups heavy cream
¼ cup sugar
Garnish:
Sweetened whipped cream
Chocolate Shavings

Crust: Preheat oven to 350°F. Butter a 9-inch springform pan
In a food processor, pulse the cookies until finely ground. Add the softened butter; pulse until evenly moistened. Press crumb mixture into the bottom and up the sides of the prepared pan to form a thin crust.

Bake 5 minutes; transfer to a rack to cool completely.

Mousse: In a food processor, combine the chocolate, vanilla and salt.

In a microwave-safe glass measure, heat 1 cup cream to just boiling. With the motor running, pour hot cream through the feed tube; process until chocolate is melted and smooth. Transfer mixture to a large bowl; cool to room temperature, stirring occasionally. In the bowl of an electric mixer beat 2 cups heavy cream with the sugar to form stiff peaks. Fold whipped cream into chocolate mixture; transfer mousse to prepared crust. Chill until set, at least 6 hours and up to overnight.

To serve: Place sweetened whipped cream in a pastry bag fitted with a medium star tip. Pipe rosettes around edge of tart. Garnish with chocolate shavings.

CHOCOLATE *Bowls* and Raspberry Sauce
[Makes 4–6 small bowls]

I love these little bowls. Try using long balloons to make banana split bowls. But a word of caution: my daughter Katie and I once dipped the balloons while the chocolate was still too warm. The result? Balloons were popping, chocolate was flying and we learned our lesson!

12-ounce bag semi-sweet or white chocolate chips
4–6 small balloons, inflated

Line a baking sheet with parchment paper; set aside.

Place chocolate chips in a microwave-safe measuring cup. Melt on defrost (or 50 percent power) for 2 minutes. Repeat in 30-second intervals until a finger pressed in the center of the chocolate can go through it, though the chocolate may not look melted, about 3 minutes total. Stir until chocolate is melted and smooth. Let cool to room temperature. Dip a balloon into the melted chocolate; twirl the balloon to create a bowl shape. Let excess drip off; place on parchment-lined baking sheet. Repeat with remaining chocolate and balloons. Chill until completely set, at least an hour and up to overnight. Snip the balloon with scissors; gently remove popped balloon. Refrigerate bowls until ready to use.

RASPBERRY SAUCE

1 16-ounce bag frozen raspberries, thawed
Sugar to taste

In a medium saucepan combine frozen raspberries with enough sugar to sweeten slightly, bring to a boil. Cook and stir for 1–2 minutes. Remove from heat; cool. Press through a fine mesh sieve to remove seeds.

fun

with

chocolate

ICE *Bowls* with Sorbet

Make ahead: Ice bowls can be made several days in advance. Store unmolded bowls in Ziploc bags in the freezer. Don't make too far ahead or the ice will begin to shrink and expose the items frozen inside.

Tip: During the winter months freeze plain water in the bowls. Place a lit votive in each cup and use to line a walkway for a special party.

No recipe here, just inspiration. Ice bowls are a beautiful way to serve sorbet, shrimp cocktail, oysters or anything that you want to serve very cold. You'll need custard cups in two sizes. Place flower petals, fresh herbs or lemon, lime or orange slices in the larger cup. Place a smaller custard cup inside. Carefully fill the space between the 2 bowls with water. If any of the filling materials float up and out of the water, poke them back down with a toothpick. Don't try to control the way the items freeze in the water—I've learned through the years that is doesn't matter if you fuss with them or not, they always turn out beautifully. Place the cups on a sheet tray on a level shelf in the freezer. Freeze until solid. To unmold, hold upside down under running water and gently twist the cups to release.

To serve: Ice bowls can slide around on the plate, so place a lettuce leaf or decorative cocktail napkin underneath.

LIMONCELLO
[Makes about 3 quarts]

sleep time: **One month**

I have been lucky enough to lead some wonderful cooking tours through Italy. On one trip I introduced my traveling companions to the joys of limoncello. Here's an easy version to make at home— and a toast to Lucia, Moritzia, Marta, Carolina and Erika: Ciao Bellas!

Tip: Homemade Limoncello makes a great gift. Plan ahead for the holidays and look for pretty and unusual bottles to package it in.

15 organic lemons
2 bottles (750 ml each) good quality, 100 proof vodka or grain alcohol
4½ cups sugar
5 cups water

Wash the lemons in hot water, scrubbing thoroughly. With a vegetable peeler, remove the peel. Scrape away all the white pith on the back of the peel with a knife. Put the peels in a 4-quart Mason jar. Add 1 bottle of Vodka; stir. Seal the jar. Place in a dark cabinet for at least 2 weeks and up to a month.

After at least 2 weeks and up to a month, take out the lemon-Vodka mixture. In a sauce pan over high heat, stir the sugar and water together; boil for 5 minutes. Let the sugar syrup cool completely in the pan, about 10 minutes. Add the sugar syrup to the lemon-Vodka mixture. Stir in the second bottle of Vodka. Re-seal the jar; return to the cabinet for 2 more weeks. Strain the mixture; discard the lemon peel. Pour into clean bottles with caps or corks. Keep a bottle in the freezer until ready to use. (Store extra bottles in the pantry.) Serve, icy cold, in vodka or shot glasses.

raise

a

toast

AVOCADO
Chicken and Black Bean Enchiladas with Rose's Green
  Salsa and Guacamole, 76

ALMOND
Almond Shortcakes with Double Cream
  and Triple Berries, 108

ALMOND PASTE
Cherry Almond Apricot Tart, 106

APPLE
Baked Cinnamon Apple Pancake, 4

APRICOT
Cherry Almond Apricot Tart, 106

BANANA
Buttermilk Banana Cake with Cream Cheese
  Cloud Frosting, 114

BBQ
BBQ Chicken Pizza, 84
Asian BBQ Ribs, 86

BEANS
Black Bean with Bacon Soup, 42
Chicken and Black Bean Enchiladas with Rose's Green
  Salsa and Guacamole, 76
Chili with Sausage and Beef, 94
Roasted Red Skin and Green Bean Salad, 50
Tortilla Soup, 38

BEEF
Beef Fajitas with Peppers and Onions, 92
Beef Tenderloin with Horseradish Sauce, 88
Beef Tenderloin Stew, 90
Chili with Sausage and Beef, 94
Italian Wedding Soup, 40
Mini Ruebens in Rye Cups, 30
Rosemary Roast Beef Crostini, 28

BERRIES
Lemon Buttermilk Waffles with Blueberry Sauce, 2
Fruit Flower Kabobs in Wheat Grass, 16
Lemon Panna Cotta with Berry Sauce, 100
Almond Shortcakes with Double Cream
  and Triple Berries, 108

BLUE CHEESE
Blue Cheese Butter, 89
Rosemary Roast Beef Crostini, 28

Rough-cut Cole Slaw with Blue Cheese, 52
Spinach Salad with Red Currant Dressing,
  Gorgonzola and Sweet and Spicy Nuts, 44

BOURSIN
Boursin-filled Peppadews, 32
Salmon in Phyllo with Lemon and Herbs, 68

BOURBON
Spiced Pumpkin Pie with Bourbon Cream, 110

BRANDY
Caramel Crepes, 112

BREAD
Creamy Corn Bread and Honey Butter, 39
Great Garlic Bread, 41
Mini Ruebens in Rye Cups, 30

BREAKFAST
Baked Cinnamon Apple Pancake, 4
Cherry Butter, 14
Cinnamon Sugar Churros, 12
Fruit and Nut Granola, 6
Fruit Flower Kabobs in Wheat Grass, 16
Lemon Buttermilk Waffles with Blueberry Sauce, 2
Spicy Breakfast Burritos, 8
Tequila-spiked Fruit Salad with Lime, 10

BRIE
Wine Glazed Brie with Flower Petal Mosaic, 22

BUTTER
Blue Cheese Butter, 89
Cherry Butter, 14
Creamy Corn Bread and Honey Butter, 39
Grilled Corn with Roasted Garlic Butter, 56

CABBAGE
Rough-cut Cole Slaw with Blue Cheese, 52

CAKE
Buttermilk Banana Cake with Cream Cheese
  Cloud Frosting, 114
Creamy Cheesecake , 116

CAPERS
Chicken Piccatta, 80
Smoked Salmon Puff Pastry Pizza
  with Capers and Dill, 26

CARAMEL
Caramel Crepes, 112

CHERRY
Cherry Butter, 14
Cherry Almond Apricot Tart, 106
Mustard Pork Tenderloin with Cherry
   Cabernet Sauce, 96

CHICKEN
Asian Chicken Salad on Endive Spears, 24
BBQ Chicken Pizza, 84
Chicken and Black Bean Enchiladas with Rose's
   Green Salsa and Guacamole, 76
Chicken Piccatta, 80
Macadamia Chicken with Mango Butter Sauce, 82
Tortilla Soup, 38

CHOCOLATE
Chocolate Bowls, 120
Double Chocolate Mousse Tart
with Cookie Crust, 118

CHORIZO
Spicy Breakfast Burritos, 8

COGNAC
Caramel Crepes, 112

COLE SLAW
Rough-cut Cole Slaw with Blue Cheese, 52

CORN
Grilled Corn with Roasted Garlic Butter, 56

CREAM CHEESE
Buttermilk Banana Cake with Cream Cheese
   Cloud Frosting, 114
Cherry Butter, 14
Creamy Cheesecake, 116

CRÈME FRAICHE
Almond Shortcakes with Double Cream
   and Triple Berries, 108
Lemon Panna Cotta with Berry Sauce, 100

CREPES
Caramel Crepes, 112

CROSTINI
Rosemary Roast Beef Crostini, 28

CRUDITE
Garden Vegetable Basket, 34

DESSERTS
Almond Shortcakes with Double Cream
   and Triple Berries, 108
Buttermilk Banana Cake with Cream Cheese
   Cloud Frosting, 114

Caramel Crepes with Brandied Caramel Sauce
   and Toasted Pecans, 112
Cherry Almond Apricot Tart, 106
Chocolate Bowls and Raspberry Sauce, 120
Creamy Cheesecake, 116
Double Chocolate Mousse Tart with Chocolate
   Cookie Crust, 118
Fruit Tart with Gingersnap Cookie Crust, 104
Ice Bowls with Sorbet, 122
Lemon Panna Cotta with Berry Sauce, 100
Limoncello, 124
Peaches in Wine, 102
Spiced Pumpkin Pie with Bourbon Cream, 110

DONUT
Cinnamon Sugar Churros, 12

EGGS
Spicy Breakfast Burritos, 8

EGGPLANT
Open Faced Ratatouille Sandwiches
   with Gruyere, 64

ENTREES
Asian BBQ Ribs, 86
Baked Macaroni and Cheese with Buttered
   Crumb Topping, 74
BBQ Chicken Pizza, 84
Beef Fajitas with Peppers and Onions, 92
Beef Tenderloin Stew, 90
Beef Tenderloin with Horseradish Sauce, 88
Chicken and Black Bean Enchiladas with Rose's
   Green Salsa and Guacamole, 76
Chicken Piccatta, 80
Chili with Sausage and Beef, 94
Creole Pasta, 72
Macadamia Chicken with Mango Butter Sauce, 82
Mustard Pork Tenderloin with Cherry
   Cabernet Sauce, 96
Open Faced Ratatouille Sandwiches
   with Gruyere, 64
Salmon in Phyllo with Lemon and Herbs, 68
Seafood Stew, 70
Stuffed Italian Sandwich, 66

FAJITAS
Beef Fajitas with Peppers and Onions, 92

FISH
Salmon in Phyllo with Lemon and Herbs, 68
Seafood Stew, 70
Seared Peppered Tuna with Pickled Cucumber, 20
Smoked Salmon Puff Pastry Pizza with
   Capers and Dill, 26

FLOWERS
Fruit Flower Kabobs in Wheat Grass, 16
Wine Glazed Brie with Flower Petal Mosaic, 22

FROSTING
Buttermilk Banana Cake with Cream Cheese
  Cloud Frosting, 114

FRUIT
Fruit Flower Kabobs in Wheat Grass, 16
Fruit Tart with Gingersnap Cookie Crust, 104
Peaches in Wine, 102
Tequila-spiked Fruit Salad with Lime, 10

HELLMICH, CHEF STEVE
Double Chocolate Mousse Tart
with Cookie Crust, 118

HORS D' OEUVRES
Asian Chicken Salad on Endive Spears, 24
Boursin-filled Peppadews, 32
Garden Vegetable Basket, 34
Mini Ruebens in Rye Cups, 30
Rosemary Roast Beef Crostini, 28
Seared Peppered Tuna with Pickled Cucumber, 20
Smoked Salmon Puff Pastry Pizza
  with Capers and Dill, 26
Wine Glazed Brie with Flower Petal Mosaic, 22

HORSERADISH
Beef Tenderloin with Horseradish Sauce, 88

LEMON
Chicken Piccatta, 80
Lemon Buttermilk Waffles with Blueberry Sauce, 2
Lemon Panna Cotta with Berry Sauce, 100

LIME
Tequila-spiked Fruit Salad with Lime, 10

LISS, TRINA
Creamy Cheesecake, 116

LONG, BECKY
Spicy Breakfast Burritos, 8

MASCARPONE
Fruit Tart with Gingersnap Cookie Crust, 104

NUTS
Asian Chicken Salad on Endive Spears, 24
Buttermilk Banana Cake with Cream Cheese
  Cloud Frosting, 114
Caramel Crepes, 112
Fruit and Nut Granola, 6
Macadamia Chicken with Mango Butter Sauce, 82
Spiced Pumpkin Pie with Bourbon Cream, 110
Spinach Salad with Red Currant Dressing,
  Gorgonzola and Sweet and Spicy Nuts, 44

PANCAKE
Baked Cinnamon Apple Pancake, 4

PASTA
Baked Macaroni and Cheese with Buttered
  Crumb Topping, 74
Creole Pasta, 72
Italian Wedding Soup, 40

PEPPADEW
Boursin-filled Peppadews, 32

POPPYSEED
Lemon Buttermilk Waffles with Blueberry Sauce, 2

PORK
Asian BBQ Ribs, 86
Italian Wedding Soup, 40
Mustard Pork Tenderloin with Cherry
  Cabernet Sauce, 96

POTATOES
Mushroom Potatoes, 54
Roasted Red Skin and Green Bean Salad, 50

PHYLLO
Salmon in Phyllo with Lemon and Herbs, 68

PIZZA
BBQ Chicken Pizza, 84
Smoked Salmon Puff Pastry Pizza with
  Capers and Dill, 26

PUMPKIN
Spiced Pumpkin Pie with Bourbon Cream, 110

RASPBERRY
Creamy Cheesecake, 116
Raspberry Sauce, 120

RATATOUILLE
Open Faced Ratatouille Sandwiches
  with Gruyere, 64

SALADS
Chop-Chop Salad, 48
Roasted Red Skin and Green Bean Salad, 50
Rough-cut Cole Slaw with Blue Cheese, 52
Southern Shrimp Salad, 46
Tequila-spiked Fruit Salad with Lime, 10

SALMON
Salmon in Phyllo with Lemon and Herbs, 68
Smoked Salmon Puff Pastry Pizza
  with Capers and Dill, 26

SALSA
Rose's Green Salsa and Guacamole, 78
Spicy Breakfast Burritos, 8

SANDWICHES
Open Faced Ratatouille Sandwiches
   with Gruyere, 64
Stuffed Italian Sandwich, 66

SAUCE
Beef Tenderloin with Horseradish Sauce, 88
Chicken and Black Bean Enchiladas with Rose's
   Green Salsa and Guacamole, 76
Macadamia Chicken with Mango Butter Sauce, 82
Mustard Pork Tenderloin with
   Cherry Cabernet Sauce, 96

SAUSAGE
Chili with Sausage and Beef, 94
Creole Pasta, 72
Spicy Breakfast Burritos, 8

SEAFOOD
Creole Pasta, 72
Seafood Stew, 70
Southern Shrimp Salad, 46

SHORTCAKE
Almond Shortcakes with Double Cream
   and Triple Berries, 108

SHRIMP
Creole Pasta, 72
Southern Shrimp Salad, 46

SIDES
Creamed Spinach, 58
Grilled Corn with Roasted Garlic Butter, 56
Mushroom Potatoes, 54
Seasoned Onion Straws, 60

SOUP
Black Bean with Bacon Soup, 42
Italian Wedding Soup, 40
Tortilla Soup, 38

SPINACH
Creamed Spinach, 58
Spinach Salad with Red Currant Dressing,
   Gorgonzola and Sweet and Spicy Nuts, 44

STEW
Beef Tenderloin Stew, 90
Seafood Stew, 70

TART
Cherry Almond Apricot Tart, 106
Double Chocolate Mousse Tart
   with Cookie Crust, 118

TEAL, CHEF PAUL
Seared Peppered Tuna with Pickled Cucumber, 20

TEQUILA
Tequila-spiked Fruit Salad with Lime, 10

TOMATILLO
Rose's Green Salsa and Guacamole, 76

TORTILLAS
Beef Fajitas with Peppers and Onions, 92
Chicken and Black Bean Enchiladas with Rose's
   Green Salsa and Guacamole, 76
Spicy Breakfast Burritos, 8
Tortilla Soup, 38

TUNA
Seared Peppered Tuna with Pickled Cucumber, 20

VEAL
Italian Wedding Soup, 40

WAFFLE
Lemon Buttermilk Waffles with Blueberry Sauce, 2

For additional recipes, ideas and tips,
visit www.amystable.com

To order additional copies
visit www.orangefrazer.com